Martha Stewart's
Slow Cooker

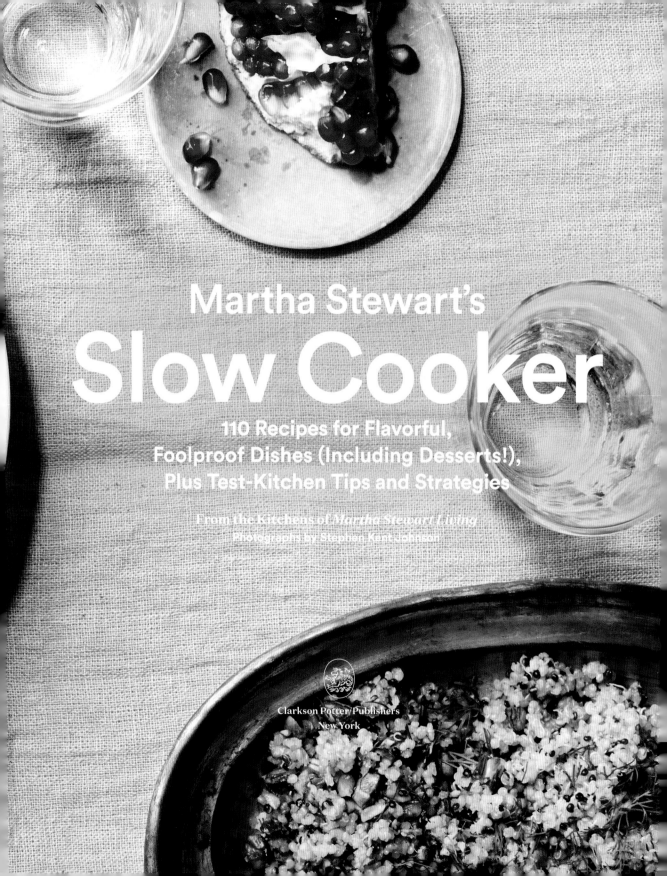

Martha Stewart's
Slow Cooker

110 Recipes for Flavorful, Foolproof Dishes (Including Desserts!), Plus Test-Kitchen Tips and Strategies

From the kitchens of *Martha Stewart Living*
Photographs by Stephen Kent Johnson

Clarkson Potter/Publishers
New York

With thanks to the creative, hard-working team who put this book together: Ellen Morrissey, Susanne Ruppert, Michele Outland, Frances Boswell, Stephen Kent Johnson, Grace Parisi, Melissa Schreiber, Ayesha Patel, Rory Evans, John Myers, Ava Pollack, Bridget Fitzgerald, Nanette Maxim, Denise Ginley, Kavita Thirupuvanam, Sarah Carey, Gertrude Porter, Josefa Palacios, Aida Ibarra, Caitlin Brown, Hilary Valentine, Mike Varrassi, Stacey Tyrell, Jeanine Robinson, Brandon Harrison, Ashley Phillips Meyer, Debbie Glasserman, Marysarah Quinn, Linnea Knollmueller, Mark McCauslin, Aaron Wehner, Doris Cooper, Kate Tyler, Stephanie Davis, and Jana Branson.

Library of Congress Cataloging- in-Publication Data

Names: Stewart, Martha.

Title: Martha Stewart's slow cooker: 110 recipes for flavorful, foolproof dishes (including desserts!), plus test-kitchen tips and strategies / editors of Martha Stewart Living; photographs by Stephen Kent Johnson.

Other titles: Slow cooker | Martha Stewart Living.

Description: First edition. | New York : Clarkson Potter/Publishers, [2017] | Includes index.

Identifiers: LCCN 2016051525| ISBN 9780307954688 (trade pbk.) | ISBN 9780307954695 (eISBN)

Subjects: LCSH: Electric cooking, Slow. | Cooking, American. | LCGFT: Cookbooks.

Classification: LCC TX827. M37 2017 | DDC 641.5/86— dc23

LC record available at https://lccn.loc. gov/2016051525.

ISBN 978-0-307-95468-8
Ebook ISBN 978-0-307-95469-5

Printed in China

Design by Michele Outland

Photographs by Stephen Kent Johnson

10 9 8 7 6 5 4 3 2 1

First Edition

To all of us who want to save time to
make time to spend with those we love!

Foreword

To tell the honest truth, I have never, ever, really used a slow cooker—that is until now! I was not brought up by a mother who relied on anything except her collection of favorite stainless-steel pots and cast-iron skillets, her stovetop pressure cooker, and her enamel-coated roasting pans. Mother's favorite electric appliances were her white four-and-a-half-quart stand mixer, her handheld electric mixer, and her blender. We talked about slow cookers but never relied on one. In retrospect, we missed out!

After months of recipe developing and testing, and being more and more impressed with the attributes of the several different slow cookers we bought for the test kitchen, I am a total convert. What we found was that with a bit of clever tweaking, and an added step or two prior to placing the food in the cooker or after taking it out, results were nothing short of spectacular. Braising, steaming, simmering, poaching, boiling, even baking—each can be accomplished with panache and expertise, resulting in dishes with delightful textures and tastes. And with a few colorful garnishes and other finishes, the appearance of each dish can be pleasing, too.

I know that once you try one of our recipes, you will reach for this book time and time again and serve many memorable meals to your family and friends. Imagine Chinese congee, a savory rice porridge, cooked effortlessly in the machine; or scalloped potatoes, cooked to creamy perfection; or sweet potatoes, roasted slowly until meltingly tender. And please, please, try the extra-delicious barley risotto with mushrooms, the hearty bouillabaisse, and especially, my favorite, the Japanese custard known as chawanmushi.

"Slow cooker" cooking? How about "smart cooker" cooking. Enjoy!

Martha Stewart

Braised Baby
Artichokes,
page 192

Brisket and Onions,
page 20

The Basics

Although it's known as a slow cooker, we prefer to think of this countertop wonder as a *smart* cooker. Yes, over the decades it has more than earned its reputation for getting dinner on the table on hectic weeknights. But its genius extends well beyond being a Monday through Friday MVP, as we happily discovered while developing and testing the recipes in this book. If you've only ever used the slow cooker for fix-it-and-forget-it dinners, you are missing out—on so many good meals, great flavors, and *aha!* moments. In fact, the recipes here may completely recalibrate how you think about the machine. They play to the appliance's strengths: Soups, stews, and chilis, of course, are perfect after hours of low heat. But bear in mind, too, that in the slow cooker, tough, inexpensive cuts of meat—like brisket and lamb shanks—and even hearty vegetables (think autumn squash) braise to tender perfection without a lot of (or even a little) babysitting.

The recipes also show you how to skirt the machine's weaknesses, like watered-down flavors or the overall mushiness that can come from long, low-temperature heat. For example, quickly searing meat beforehand creates a flavor base and helps it maintain texture once it's transferred to the slow cooker. Conversely, a few minutes under the broiler after many hours in the cooker will crisp up chicken skin or give ribs that satisfying, sticky-glaze finish.

Perhaps most impressive, the *slow* in slow cooker can at times be a misnomer—some dishes, like poached salmon, cook in just an hour! (In this case, it's the foolproof technique, not the time factor we're after.) The good news here is that using the machine reduces the risk of overcooking a nice piece of fish.

Once you reset how you think about the slow cooker, opportunities for ingenuity abound. For instance, recipes that call for a bain-marie (essentially a water bath) will no longer seem fussy when you can simply place a pan in a half-inch of water in your slow cooker, then slice into a perfectly moist cheesecake a few hours later. On Thanksgiving, with a full oven and a crowded stovetop, you'll wisely press your slow cooker into service for scalloped potatoes or braised red cabbage. And on those stifling summer days—when you have a bushel of the most glorious fruit but a kitchen that's simply too hot to breathe in, let alone turn on the oven—a low-heat slow cooker is the secret weapon for making an irresistible blueberry cornmeal buckle or a peach crisp.

So take another look at your slow cooker and consider it for more than your crowd-pleasing chili. Cook your way through this book, and don't be surprised when you fall in love—quickly—with this new, smarter approach to slow cooking.

Slow Cooker Commandments

For more than a year, our editors and recipe developers embraced the task of creating recipes that maximize all the slow cooker's assets and make up for some of its well-known limitations. At the same time, they heartily took on the challenge of adapting many of our favorite dishes to the machine's distinctive cooking method. In doing so, they became quite enamored—you could say surprisingly so—of the appliance that's long been loved by legions of home cooks. Our cooks researched, read up, dug in, and, more than anything, rolled up their sleeves and got into the kitchen to figure out what the slow cooker is good at, what it's great at, and—at times—where the pitfalls lie. After that intensive study, and the intensive tasting and tweaking that went along with it, here are our so-called commandments:

1 **Forget about "forgetting it."** We got better results when we didn't simply turn on the switch and walk away for the day. While the appliance is known for cooking weeknight dinners, we really loved it for preparing big-batch recipes on weekends—the kinds of afternoons when you're in and out of the house on errands. Great results came with being mindful of what was in the pot, when we could occasionally open the lid and give it a stir (bottom line: not often), and which heat setting would result in the very best flavors and textures.

2 **Don't just dump it in.** Simply scraping chopped vegetables and some meat straight from the cutting board into the pot with a handful of dried seasonings might not taste so good six hours from now. Invest 10 to 20 minutes at the start of the process: Go ahead and sauté those onions, carrots, and celery, and don't skip the step of browning that roast (on all sides!); this will encourage the flavors to develop more fully and get richer with time.

3 **Be wary of too many shortcuts.** In researching popular slow-cooker recipes, some struck us as a mash-up of processed, packaged foods—like instant gravy mix stirred into canned soup topped with a packet of powdered salad dressing! Not surprisingly, we found the best flavors resulted from using the freshest ingredients. The shortcut we relied on first and foremost was the slow cooker itself.

4 **Relax and let the machine take charge.** The slow cooker is a refuge for the impatient. Maybe you are the type of cook who is always trying to rush things—"simmer" to you means a low boil, or you occasionally burn onions in an (admittedly too hasty) effort to caramelize them, or you have ruined a pan or two with scorched sauces. If that sounds familiar, you'll be relieved to know you can trust this appliance to perfectly poach fish and poultry and caramelize onions and simmer sauces without constant checking and stirring.

5 **Let texture guide you.** Select tough, inexpensive cuts of meat that stand up to slow, steady, moist heat (pork shoulder, beef brisket, and lamb shanks are great for long braising; prime rib, not so much). Avoid anything that cooks quickly and perfectly on the stovetop or grill—in other words, tender chops and other lean meats. Root vegetables, too, develop great flavor and maintain their shape and much of their hardiness in the slow cooker, while many delicate vegetables are still best simply—and briefly—steamed on the stove.

6 **Cook once, serve multiple meals.** The slow cooker lets you prepare ahead and jump-start dinners throughout the week. Braise a pork shoulder to make porchetta, for example, and—depending on your last-minute prep, condiments, and an array of garnishes and toppings—you can serve it on a platter with fresh tomatoes and salsa verde one night, in sandwiches with garlicky greens the next, or over creamy polenta, and so on.

7 **Finish with lots of color—and some crunch.** For the most satisfying meals, round out the slow-cooked main course with fresh herbs and vegetables, mixed greens, or diced onion. These toppings and sides bring welcome texture and snap.

8 **Deploy the machine as a space saver.** When your oven is crowded with the main course (like a holiday roast) and casseroles or even desserts, use the slow cooker for sides, such as potatoes or squash. When your stovetop is fully engaged, let the slow cooker step in as a low burner. (It can also be used to reheat mashed potatoes, say, or as a warming dish for cooked pasta.)

9 **Keep your cool.** You might think of autumn and winter as slow-cooker season, but the machine especially shines in the hot summer months, because you can cook dinner without heating up the kitchen. Beer-braised pork ribs only sound like they came off the backyard grill—make them in the slow cooker and serve with chilled slaw, potato salad, and more beer (!) on a steamy summer night.

10 **Realize how sweet it is!** The slow cooker may be known for savory foods, but it also turns out excellent desserts—custards and puddings, fruit crisps and buckles, even cheesecake! Keep in mind that unlike soups or stews, "baking" in a slow cooker needs to be watched a bit more closely. Depending on the strength of your machine, the batter may be more or less cooked in the time suggested. It's particularly great for custards and puddings when you use it as a bain-marie. You are just one slow cooker (and a butane torch) away from crème brûlée!

How to Use a Slow Cooker

The popularity of the slow cooker first heated up in the 1970s, as it gained legions of fans for its ability to conveniently get meals to the table. The machines of that time were decidedly no-frills, with a ceramic pot and perhaps high and low heat settings.

While plenty of cooks are still turning out dinner night after night with those first models, the designs have come a long way in recent years: If you haven't upgraded in the past decade, consider doing so—and find a machine with the exact options that suit the way you cook. For instance, some machines feature the dual function of cooking rice and slow cooking; others, known as multi-cookers, offer pressure-cooking options as well. We like models with cast aluminum or nonstick inserts that can go from the stovetop (where you can sauté vegetables or brown meat to build a foundation of flavor) into the slow cooker, thereby limiting the need to wash more dishes. If you have such a model, adjust our recipes to use your insert rather than the skillet or other pan called for in the first steps. For all the bells and whistles you can get, the one extra we recommend most is really rather simple: a timer control. This feature lets you program a heat adjustment, moving from high to low, or just maintaining low heat to keep the food warm. (This last option is especially important when you're following a recipe that calls for cooking on low for six hours, but you know you'll be out of the house for nine hours.)

Even a brand-new slow cooker will require a getting-to-know-you phase, as you figure out its particular strengths and idiosyncrasies. Start, of course, with a careful perusal of the manual (seriously—it's not all dire warnings about shock hazards!); then start experimenting with simple recipes and affordable ingredients. Try cooking dishes you are familiar with, so you can compare the slow cooker's results to how a recipe turns out when you cook it conventionally.

In general, recipes cooked in the slow cooker on the high setting take half the time of those on the low setting. However, low heat is preferred for many recipes so as to allow flavors to combine and develop, and in some cases, to maintain the proper texture of the food as it cooks. High heat can cause some dishes to fall apart too quickly. In most recipes in this book, our recommended heat setting is listed first, followed by the alternate setting and time. You'll find some instances where only one setting is recommended, so please take heed and stick to those instructions, for best results.

Here are some other suggestions to keep in mind:

- **Preheat the machine while you prepare aromatics or sear meat.** Our recipe developers got great results when they turned the machine (with the insert in it) to the high setting for about 20 minutes. They also got better results when they added hot (or even boiling) liquids to the recipes at the start. Flavors start building early on in the slow cooker, and working with hot ingredients and a warm machine can help give them a head start.

- **Prep the insert.** A thin coat of either vegetable oil or softened butter will make cleanup so much easier. This is particularly important for baked dishes.

- **Fill it with just the right amount.** The ideal capacity is two-thirds full. Anything less, and the food can scorch or burn (yes, it can happen even in a slow cooker!), and anything more can compromise how evenly the food cooks. If you don't have enough food in the insert, consider reducing the cooking time.

- **Watch out for hot spots.** Many machines have a hot spot along the back wall, which can cause uneven cooking (or worse, burning) over long periods of time. You may want to rotate the insert within the cooker every hour or so to avoid overcooked spots—especially when baking treats like cinnamon buns and apple crisp. (It's a good idea to press a piece of foil against the usual hot spot area, then spray or brush it with vegetable oil.)

- **Put a sling in it.** When you need to lift something out of the insert after cooking—such as a meatloaf—start by making a foil sling: Fold two 30-inch lengths of aluminum foil in half lengthwise, twice, into two 30-inch-long, 4-ply strips. Crisscross the strips to cover the bottom and sides of the slow cooker insert, allowing excess foil to overhang. Spray or brush the foil with vegetable oil, then add your ingredients.

- **Trick it out.** The machine is versatile, but at times it can need a little propping for best results. When using it as a bain-marie, for example, set some jam-jar O rings along the bottom to lift the baking dish or dishes off the surface of the insert. (Balls of aluminum foil also work.) For some recipes, you will want to wrap the lid in a clean cotton kitchen towel: The slow cooker traps moisture, which is usually a benefit—unless it means water dripping from the lid. As steam rises when you bake in the slow cooker, the towel will absorb it. This is especially helpful when making cheesecake or any other custard-based dish.

- **Be experimental.** As you get more accustomed to cooking with your machine, try adapting your favorite recipes for the slow cooker. In general, you will want to reduce any liquid by half—there's no evaporation, so you don't want to start with too much broth or water. And try this trick, especially if your cooker doesn't have the "keep warm" function: If you want the cooking to take even longer than the suggested time, put the ingredients in the insert and chill it overnight. This will generally add 60 to 90 minutes to the recipe's cooking time.

Meat

The Basics

It is the classic rags-to-riches tale, unexpectedly told by a slow cooker: The story begins with, say, a pork shoulder being placed in the crock, along with some seasonings and aromatics. Time slowly passes. Out comes something tender and rich, with a complex and well-developed flavor.

The shoulder and other tough cuts—think lamb shanks, pork butt, beef brisket, short ribs, and chuck—come from the hard-worked muscles that support the animal's weight and movement. They tend to be marbled with fat and connective tissue that, when exposed to low, slow heat, break down and render the meat moist and succulent. Yes, they're good for stovetop or conventional oven braising and stewing, but they are also perfect choices for the slow cooker (bear in mind that with the lid tightly on, moisture doesn't burn off, so sauces do not thicken as they do with braising). Leave the meat on the bone when you can, too—it will intensify the flavor as it cooks.

If you want to encourage caramelizing—and with it, the sought-after complexity of flavors—it can help to brown the meat in a skillet or Dutch oven on the stovetop before putting it into the cooker, or roast or broil it in a very hot oven for a few minutes right after it comes out. Searing meat beforehand helps it to develop a nice crust and generally improves the overall texture of the finished dish.

For all the showstopping, out-of-the-ordinary main dishes you can prepare with the slow cooker—like warming Roasted Five-Spice Pork with Udon or silky Persian Lamb Stew or Hawaiian-Style Short Ribs—don't overlook it when you're craving homey classics like Spaghetti Bolognese or Meatloaf with Balsamic Glaze. After all, the machine lends itself to a world of kitchen possibilities—newly discovered favorites and longtime familiar comforts alike.

Recipes

Brisket and Onions

Beef and Black Bean Chili

Sicilian-Style Beef Stew

Beef Stroganoff

Beef and Pork Meatballs

Carne Guisada for Tacos

French Onion Panade

Meatloaf with
Balsamic Glaze

Pho

Italian Pot Roast

Carbonnade

Ropa Vieja

Mexican Oxtail Stew

Hawaiian-Style Short Ribs

New England Boiled
Dinner

Italian Braised Pork

Pork Posole

Sausage and Vegetable
Ciambotta

Porchetta

Chickpeas with Guanciale

Spaghetti Bolognese

Marmalade and
Vinegar Pork

Beer-Braised Pork Ribs

German-Style Pork Chops

Roasted Five-Spice Pork
with Udon

Pulled Pork

Sausage Lasagna

Cassoulet

Vietnamese
Baby Back Ribs

Split Pea with Ham Soup

Choucroute Garnie

Persian Lamb Stew

Lamb with Olives
and Potatoes

This slow-cooked wonder of wonders requires just a handful of ingredients. And you can truly set it up in the morning and let it braise all day. Garnish with little more than a jar of horseradish (or the freshly grated root, if you can find it) and some fresh parsley; egg noodles are nice on the side. Brisket tastes even better when made a day or two ahead, and leftovers make the world's greatest sandwiches.

Brisket and Onions

SERVES 6

1 large onion, thinly sliced

2 garlic cloves, smashed and peeled

1 first cut of beef brisket (about 4 pounds), trimmed of excess fat

Coarse salt and freshly ground pepper

2 cups low-sodium chicken broth, store-bought or homemade (page 256)

Fresh flat-leaf parsley, for garnish

Prepared horseradish, for serving

Preheat a 5- to 6-quart slow cooker.

Combine onion and garlic in the slow cooker. Season brisket with salt and pepper, and place, fat side up, on top of onion and garlic. Add broth. Cover and cook on high until brisket is fork-tender, about 6 hours (or on low for 12 hours). Remove brisket and slice against the grain. Moisten with cooking liquid, and top with onion slices and parsley. Serve with horseradish. (Brisket can be made ahead and stored in cooking liquid, covered and refrigerated, up to 1 week. Reheat in a 300°F oven.)

Tip

A whole brisket is made up of a first cut and a second cut. For this recipe, look for the leaner first cut, or "flat cut." Ask your butcher to trim the layer of fat on the brisket down to ¼ inch, which is enough to keep the meat moist and tender as it cooks.

True Texas chili is widely recognized as a bowl of beef chuck that has been seasoned with dried chiles, tomatoes, and spices and simmered until it's meltingly tender. Beans, if included at all, are most often pintos. This recipe swaps in black beans for variety and chili powder (a mix of ground chiles and spices such as oregano and cumin) for convenience.

Beef and Black Bean Chili

SERVES 4

1 cup dried black beans, picked over and rinsed

1 pound beef chuck, cut into ¾-inch chunks

1 can (15 ounces) tomato puree

1 red onion, finely chopped

2 garlic cloves, minced

3 tablespoons chili powder

2 cups hot water

Coarse salt and freshly ground pepper

Sour cream, diced jalapeño, chopped avocado, and grated cheddar cheese or crumbled queso fresco, for serving

Place beans in a bowl; cover with water by several inches. Refrigerate, covered, overnight; drain. (To quick soak, cover beans in a large saucepan with water. Bring to a boil. Remove from heat. Let stand, covered, for 1 hour; drain.)

Preheat a 5- to 6-quart slow cooker.

Add beans. Add beef, tomato puree, onion (reserve 1 tablespoon for garnish), garlic, chili powder, the hot water, 2 teaspoons salt, and ½ teaspoon pepper and stir to combine. Cover and cook on high until chili has thickened and beans are tender, 6 hours (or on low for 8 hours). Serve with sour cream, reserved onion, jalapeño, avocado, and cheese.

Mediterranean flavors—tomatoes, shallots, fennel, rosemary, orange zest, green olives, and red wine—abound in this standout supper. In testing, we found that the beef chuck tasted better when we seasoned it with salt and let it sit overnight in the refrigerator before cooking. We like to serve it over olive-oil mashed potatoes, with more red wine alongside.

Sicilian-Style Beef Stew

SERVES 4 TO 6

3 pounds beef chuck, fat trimmed, meat cut into 1½-inch pieces

Coarse salt and freshly ground pepper

2 tablespoons extra-virgin olive oil

6 shallots, thinly sliced

½ cup dry red wine

1 can (28 ounces) whole peeled tomatoes with their juices

1 fennel bulb, cut into ½-inch wedges

1 rosemary sprig

2 (1-inch) strips orange zest, plus wedges for serving

1 cup pitted green olives, such as Castelvetrano

Preheat a 5- to 6-quart slow cooker.

Season beef with salt and pepper. Heat a large skillet over medium-high. Add 1 tablespoon oil and half the beef in a single layer; cook, turning a few times, until browned, 5 to 7 minutes. Transfer to the slow cooker. Repeat with remaining oil and beef.

Add shallots and wine to skillet; cook, scraping up any browned bits with a wooden spoon, until wine has almost evaporated, about 3 minutes. Transfer to slow cooker. Crush tomatoes and stir in with their juices, fennel, rosemary, and zest. Cover and cook on high until meat is fork-tender, about 4½ hours (or on low for 9 hours).

Stir in olives, and season with salt and pepper. Remove rosemary sprig, and serve stew with orange wedges.

You'll notice an interesting trick in our recipe for this favorite. After the meat and vegetables are cooked for several hours, we make a slurry and boil it very briefly (one minute!), just until thickened. Then it is stirred into the meat mixture, off the heat, with sour cream and mustard, for a luxuriously creamy finish that you wouldn't get from the slow cooker itself.

Beef Stroganoff

SERVES 8

2 pounds beef chuck, trimmed of excess fat and sliced (about ½ inch thick and 3 inches long)

1 large onion, chopped

1 pound white mushrooms, trimmed and halved or quartered, if large

Coarse salt and freshly ground pepper

2 tablespoons cornstarch

2 tablespoons boiling water

½ cup sour cream

2 tablespoons Dijon mustard

Cooked egg noodles, for serving

Chopped fresh dill, for serving

Preheat a 5- to 6-quart slow cooker.

Place beef, onion, mushrooms, 1½ teaspoons salt, and ¼ teaspoon pepper in the slow cooker; toss to combine. Cover and cook on low until meat is tender, about 8 hours (or on high for 6 hours).

In a heatproof measuring cup, whisk cornstarch with the water. Ladle 1 cup cooking liquid into measuring cup; whisk to combine. Pour into a small saucepan; bring to a boil. Cook until thickened, about 1 minute. With slow cooker turned off, stir in cornstarch mixture, then sour cream and mustard. Serve beef over egg noodles and top with dill.

Making meatballs in the slow cooker is not all that different from cooking them on the stovetop, but it's worth keeping in mind when you want to tote them along to a potluck, or simply when all the burners are occupied.

Beef and Pork Meatballs

SERVES 4 TO 6

FOR MEATBALLS

- 8 ounces ground beef chuck
- 8 ounces ground pork
- 1 garlic clove, minced
- ½ cup finely grated Parmigiano-Reggiano, plus more for garnish
- 3 tablespoons finely chopped fresh flat-leaf parsley
- 2 large eggs, lightly beaten
- Coarse salt and freshly ground black pepper
- 1½ slices white bread, torn into pieces
- ¼ cup milk
- 3 tablespoons extra-virgin olive oil

FOR SAUCE

- 1 tablespoon extra-virgin olive oil
- ½ small red onion, finely chopped
- 3 garlic cloves, minced
- 2 tablespoons tomato paste
- 1 can (28 ounces) peeled plum tomatoes with juices, pureed
- 12 fresh basil leaves, torn
- ¼ teaspoon dried oregano
- Pinch red-pepper flakes (optional)
- Coarse salt and freshly ground black pepper

Make meatballs: Mix beef and pork, using your hands. Mix in garlic, cheese, parsley, eggs, and 1¼ teaspoons salt; season with pepper. Soak bread in milk for 5 minutes, then mix into meat mixture. With dampened hands or an ice-cream scoop, roll mixture into 1½-inch balls, transferring to a rimmed baking sheet as you work.

Preheat a 5- to 6-quart slow cooker.

Heat 3 tablespoons oil in a heavy skillet over medium-high. Working in batches, fry meatballs, shaking skillet occasionally, until brown all over, about 6 minutes. With a slotted spoon, transfer to a large bowl.

Make sauce: Heat oil in same skillet over medium. Add onion and garlic, stirring occasionally, until tender, about 5 minutes. Stir in tomato paste and cook 3 minutes. Add pureed tomatoes, basil, oregano, red-pepper flakes (if using), and ½ teaspoon salt. Season with black pepper and mix well to combine. Bring to a simmer.

Transfer sauce to the slow cooker. Add reserved meatballs and their juices. Cover and cook meatballs on high until cooked through, 2 hours (or on low for 4 hours). Serve meatballs and sauce with cheese.

There are a lot of variations on carne guisada, or "stewed meat." Here, cubes of chuck roast, or bottom round, are simmered with garlic, onions, and peppers in a thick tomato gravy. We like to serve it with our favorite Tex-Mex accompaniments: warm tortillas, limes, cilantro, mashed avocado, chopped radishes, corn chips, and tequila.

Carne Guisada for Tacos

SERVES 10

2½ pounds beef chuck roast or bottom round, cut into 1-inch pieces

Coarse salt and freshly ground pepper

2 tablespoons vegetable oil

1 white onion, cut into ½-inch pieces

1 green bell pepper, cut into ½-inch pieces

1 large jalapeño chile (ribs and seeds removed for less heat, if desired), cut into ¼-inch pieces

5 garlic cloves, chopped

1½ teaspoons ground cumin

¾ teaspoon chili powder

¾ teaspoon dried oregano

¼ cup plus 2 tablespoons all-purpose flour

1¾ cups low-sodium chicken broth, store-bought or homemade (page 256)

1 can (14.5 ounces) diced tomatoes

2 dried bay leaves

Warm tortillas, mashed avocado, chopped radishes, and fresh cilantro, for serving

Preheat a 5- to 6-quart slow cooker.

Season beef with salt and pepper. In a large skillet, heat 2 teaspoons oil over high. In two batches, cook beef until browned on all sides, 5 minutes per batch (add 2 teaspoons more oil for second batch). Transfer to the slow cooker.

Heat remaining 2 teaspoons oil in same skillet over medium. Cook onion, bell pepper, jalapeño, and garlic, stirring and scraping up any browned bits with a wooden spoon, until vegetables are tender, 5 minutes. Add cumin, chili powder, oregano, and flour; cook 1 minute. Slowly pour broth into skillet, stirring until liquid is smooth; simmer 2 minutes.

Transfer mixture to slow cooker, along with tomatoes and bay leaves. Season to taste with salt and pepper, and stir to combine. Cover and cook on high for 6 hours, until tender (or on low for 12 hours). Serve with tortillas, avocado, radishes, and cilantro.

Part soup, part bread pudding, this savory casserole was a test kitchen favorite when we were developing the recipes for this book. Add a salad and it makes a bistro-style main course. Keep it in mind as well when you're looking for a wonderful side dish for roasted meats and poultry; it would make a nice addition (or substitution for traditional stuffing) on any Thanksgiving table.

French Onion Panade

SERVES 4 TO 6

6 medium yellow onions, halved and sliced into half-moons (about 3¼ pounds)

2 tablespoons extra-virgin olive oil, plus more for bread

4 thyme sprigs

10 slices (½ inch thick) rustic bread

Coarse salt

2 cups beef broth, store-bought or homemade (page 257)

¼ cup dry sherry

1 bunch bitter greens, such as baby kale, washed well and trimmed (optional)

6 ounces Gruyère cheese, coarsely grated (1½ cups)

Tip
If you have an ovenproof slow-cooker insert, you can finish the dish in the oven, at 400°F, until the cheese is melted and bubbly.

Preheat a 5- to 6-quart slow cooker.

Place onions and oil in the slow cooker, and cook on high until onions are golden, about 5 hours (or on low for 10 hours).

Preheat oven to 400°F. Brush bread slices with oil and sprinkle with salt; toast until golden, about 15 minutes.

Heat broth in saucepan over medium-low until hot. Add broth, sherry, greens, and ½ teaspoon salt to slow cooker; let stand until greens wilt, about 1 minute.

Arrange bread over onions and broth. Sprinkle liberally with cheese. Cover and cook on high until cheese is melted, hot, and bubbly, about 15 minutes (or on low for 30 minutes). Serve immediately.

The trick to meatloaf is keeping it from drying out as it cooks. That's where the slow cooker comes in. It produces an utterly moist, delicious loaf that keeps for days. We love to serve it with a side of mashed potatoes, or sandwiched in slices of Pullman bread, with lettuce, tomato, and mayo.

Meatloaf with Balsamic Glaze

SERVES 6

1 pound ground beef chuck

½ pound ground pork shoulder

½ pound ground veal

1 cup fresh breadcrumbs (page 267)

1 small onion, coarsely chopped

1 carrot, coarsely chopped

1 celery stalk, coarsely chopped

2 garlic cloves, coarsely chopped

2 tablespoons unsalted butter

½ cup milk

2 large eggs, lightly beaten

¾ cup ketchup

1 tablespoon low-sodium soy sauce

2 teaspoons Dijon mustard

2 teaspoons Worcestershire sauce

2 tablespoons chopped fresh flat-leaf parsley

1 teaspoon chopped fresh thyme leaves

1 tablespoon coarse salt

1 teaspoon freshly ground pepper

1 tablespoon balsamic vinegar

3 tablespoons dark brown sugar

Preheat a 5- to 6-quart slow cooker. Make a foil sling for the slow cooker (see page 15).

In a large bowl, gently combine beef, pork, and veal with your hands; mix in breadcrumbs. Pulse onion, carrot, celery, and garlic in a food processor until finely chopped.

In a large skillet, melt butter over medium heat. Add vegetables and sauté until soft, about 5 minutes. Add milk and simmer until liquid is reduced by half, 2 to 3 minutes. Remove mixture from heat and let cool slightly.

In a bowl, combine eggs, ¼ cup ketchup, soy sauce, Dijon, Worcestershire, parsley, and thyme. Add egg mixture, cooled vegetable mixture, salt, and pepper to meat mixture; using a fork, mix just until combined (do not overmix). Form meat mixture into a 9-by-5-inch loaf. In a small bowl, whisk together remaining ½ cup ketchup, the balsamic vinegar, and brown sugar.

Transfer meatloaf to the slow cooker, spread half the glaze over meat, cover, and cook on low until internal temperature reaches 160°F on a meat thermometer, 6 hours on low (or on high for 3 hours). Uncover and spread remaining glaze over meatloaf. Cook, uncovered, until heated through, 10 to 15 minutes more. Use sling to remove meatloaf from slow cooker. Transfer meatloaf to a plate, tent with foil, and allow to rest 10 to 15 minutes before slicing and serving.

Making the broth for Vietnamese pho is an all-day affair (in the slow cooker or on the stovetop). The process is simple, however, with most of the cooking time hands-off. Cooking the thinly sliced beef occurs after you've divided it among bowls of slippery rice noodles and poured the hot broth over each serving.

Pho

SERVES 6 TO 8

4 pounds beef bones, preferably knuckle bones

2 (3-inch) cinnamon sticks

1 tablespoon coriander seeds

1 teaspoon cloves

2 cardamom pods

1 (2-inch) piece galangal, peeled and roughly chopped

1 teaspoon fennel seeds

2 whole star anise

1 large onion, quartered

1 (4-inch) piece fresh ginger, peeled and thickly sliced

6 cups boiling water

2 tablespoons Vietnamese fish sauce, such as *nuoc nam*

1 teaspoon sugar

1 pound flat rice noodles

8 ounces sirloin, flank steak, or London broil, very thinly sliced

Fresh herbs, such as mint, Thai basil, chives, and cilantro, for garnish

Limes, fresh chiles, and hot sauce (sambal oelek or Sriracha), for serving

Preheat a 5- to 6-quart slow cooker.

Bring a large stockpot filled with water to a boil. Add bones and boil 10 minutes; drain (discard cooking liquid). Rinse bones and place in the slow cooker.

Toast cinnamon, coriander, cloves, cardamom, galangal, fennel, and star anise in a small skillet on low, shaking frequently, until fragrant, about 3 minutes. Transfer spices to the slow cooker.

Return skillet to stovetop and increase heat to medium-low. Add onion and ginger, and cook until just charred. Transfer to slow cooker. Add the water, fish sauce, and sugar to slow cooker, stirring. Cover and cook on low, 8 hours (or on high for 4 hours).

Strain broth through a cheesecloth-lined sieve into a bowl (discard solids). Return pho to slow cooker and keep hot on low until ready to serve.

Meanwhile, cook rice noodles according to package instructions. Divide evenly among serving bowls. Arrange meat over noodles and ladle hot broth over top (the heat will cook the meat). Top with fresh herbs and serve with limes, chiles, and hot sauce.

Meat and potatoes, Italian style: Here a three-pound roast simmers for hours with a few pantry staples—canned tomatoes, garlic, onion, potatoes, and rosemary. The braise is so substantial, it needs nothing on the side, although a crisp green salad makes a refreshing finish.

Italian Pot Roast

SERVES 8

- 3 pounds beef chuck roast, trimmed and halved crosswise
- 4 garlic cloves, halved lengthwise
  Coarse salt and freshly ground pepper
- 1 tablespoon extra-virgin olive oil
- 1 large onion, cut into 8 wedges
- 1¼ pounds small white potatoes, scrubbed, halved if large
- 1 can (28 ounces) whole tomatoes in puree
- 1 tablespoon fresh rosemary, chopped (or 1 teaspoon dried and crumbled), plus more for garnish

Preheat a 5- to 6-quart slow cooker.

With a sharp paring knife, cut 4 slits in beef roast; stuff slits with half the garlic. Generously season beef with 1½ teaspoons salt and 1 teaspoon pepper. In a large skillet, heat oil over high, swirling to coat bottom of pan. Cook beef until browned on all sides, about 5 minutes.

In the slow cooker, combine beef, onion, potatoes, tomatoes (with puree), rosemary, and remaining garlic. Cover and cook on low until meat is fork-tender, about 8 hours (or on high for 4 hours); do not uncover while cooking.

Transfer meat to a cutting board; thinly slice and discard any gristle. Skim fat from top of sauce. To serve, divide beef and vegetables among bowls, generously spoon sauce over top, and sprinkle with chopped rosemary.

This Flemish beef stew is traditionally made with a dark Belgian-style beer, but any dark ale will do. It takes well to all kinds of accompaniments—buttered egg noodles, boiled carrots and potatoes, or a simple salad of shaved Brussels sprouts lightly dressed with olive oil and vinegar.

Carbonnade

SERVES 6 TO 8

½   pound thick-cut bacon, cut into ½-inch pieces

2   large onions, thinly sliced

2   garlic cloves, minced

1   tablespoon chopped fresh thyme leaves

3   tablespoons extra-virgin olive oil

3   pounds boneless beef chuck, cut into 1½-inch pieces

    Coarse salt and freshly ground pepper

¼   cup all-purpose flour

1   bottle (12 ounces) dark ale

1½   cups low-sodium beef broth, store-bought or homemade (page 257)

2   dried bay leaves

1½   teaspoons sugar

1   tablespoon apple cider vinegar

Preheat a 5- to 6-quart slow cooker.

In a large skillet, cook bacon on high, stirring occasionally, until crisp, about 8 minutes. Using a slotted spoon, transfer bacon to the slow cooker. Add onions, garlic, and thyme to skillet, and cook on medium-high until browned, 10 to 12 minutes. Using a slotted spoon, transfer to slow cooker. Pour off fat from skillet and add oil.

Season beef with salt and pepper, and dust with flour, shaking off excess. Heat oil on medium-high. Working in two batches, add beef and cook until browned, 8 to 10 minutes per batch. Transfer to the slow cooker and pour off fat from skillet.

Add ale to skillet and boil until reduced by half, 5 to 6 minutes; pour into slow cooker. Add broth to skillet and boil until reduced by half, 5 to 6 minutes; pour into slow cooker. Add bay leaves and sugar. Cover and cook on high until tender, 3 hours (or on low for 6 hours). Skim fat from surface and discard bay leaves. Stir in vinegar and serve.

Tip
For extra zing, stir in a tablespoon or two of Dijon mustard just before serving.

Translated from Spanish as "old clothes," this Cuban beef stew is named for its resemblance to tattered rags. Of course, the shredded and highly seasoned steak is much more tender and flavorful than its namesake, especially when served over steamed rice with a side of plantain chips.

Ropa Vieja

SERVES 6

1½ pounds flank steak

   Coarse salt and freshly
   ground pepper

2 tablespoons extra-virgin olive oil

2 onions, thickly sliced

1 large red bell pepper, thickly sliced

3 large garlic cloves, thinly sliced

1 jalapeño chile (stems and seeds
   removed for less heat, if desired),
   thinly sliced

1 tablespoon cumin seeds

2 tablespoons tomato paste

1 can (28 ounces) diced tomatoes

½ cup small Spanish olives

1 tablespoon capers, drained,
   plus 1 tablespoon brine

   Fresh cilantro leaves,
   for garnish

   Cooked white rice and
   plantain chips, for serving

Preheat a 5- to 6-quart slow cooker.

Season flank steak generously with salt and pepper. In a large skillet, heat 1 tablespoon oil over high. Add steak and cook until browned on both sides, about 8 minutes. Transfer steak to the slow cooker.

Heat remaining tablespoon oil in skillet on high. Add onions, bell pepper, garlic, jalapeño, and cumin seeds. Season with salt and pepper, and cook until tender, about 5 minutes. Stir in tomato paste and cook 2 minutes. Add tomatoes and bring to boil. Pour over steak. Cover and cook on high until very tender, 5 hours (or on low for 10 hours).

Transfer steak to a platter and cut in half crosswise. Using two forks, shred meat. Transfer sauce to skillet and cook on high until slightly thickened, 10 minutes. Stir in shredded meat, olives, and capers with brine; cook until heated through, 2 minutes. Top with cilantro and serve with rice and plantain chips.

Like many inexpensive cuts, oxtail cooks beautifully in the slow cooker. The meat needs lots of moisture—and lots of time—to bring out the best flavors and textures. This flavorful stew is further enhanced by Mexican seasonings (dried chiles and fresh epazote) and a few fresh vegetables.

Mexican Oxtail Stew

SERVES 6 TO 8

1½ pounds boneless beef chuck, trimmed of fat and cut into 1½-inch chunks

1½ pounds oxtail, trimmed of fat and cut into 2-inch pieces

3 quarts boiling water, plus more for chiles

Coarse salt and ground pepper

2 onions, finely chopped

6 garlic cloves, minced

3 bay leaves

¼ teaspoon ground cumin

⅛ teaspoon ground cloves

¾ ounce dried guajillo chiles, stemmed and seeded

¾ ounce dried ancho chiles, stemmed and seeded

1 large tomato, coarsely chopped

6 sprigs epazote or cilantro, plus more for serving

1 small acorn squash, halved, seeded, and sliced into thin wedges

2 carrots, halved and quartered

¼ pound green beans, trimmed and cut in half

2 ears corn, cut into 1-inch pieces

Warm tortillas, diced white onion, and lime wedges, for serving

Preheat a 5- to 6-quart slow cooker.

Place beef, oxtail, and 3 quarts boiling water in the slow cooker and cook on high 1 hour (do not cook on low). With a slotted spoon, skim foam from surface. Add 2 teaspoons salt, onions, garlic, bay leaves, cumin, cloves, and ¼ teaspoon pepper, and cook 2 hours more.

Meanwhile, in a heavy skillet over medium heat, toast guajillo and ancho chiles until just fragrant, a few seconds per side. Transfer to a bowl and cover with boiling water. Let stand until softened, 15 to 20 minutes. Drain chiles, reserving ¼ cup soaking liquid. Transfer to blender. Add tomato, epazote, and reserved soaking liquid; blend until smooth.

Stir chile mixture into stew. Add squash and carrots, and cook until tender, about 1 hour. Skim off fat. Add beans and corn, and cook 20 minutes. Discard bay leaves. Season with salt and pepper. Serve immediately with tortillas, diced onion, lime, and epazote.

Have your butcher cut flanken-style short ribs for this sweet and spicy dish, typical of the Hawaiian Islands. The ribs are cut across the bones instead of between them; they must be cooked in liquid over a long period of time to achieve the requisite "falling off the bone" texture.

Hawaiian-Style Short Ribs

SERVES 6

2 red onions, cut into 1-inch wedges, root ends left intact

4 garlic cloves, smashed and peeled

1 (2-inch) piece fresh ginger, peeled and thinly sliced

4 pounds bone-in beef short ribs (about 6), cut into 3½-inch pieces

1½ cups packed dark brown sugar

1 cup low-sodium soy sauce

¼ cup plus 2 tablespoons rice vinegar

1 tablespoon hot sauce, such as Sriracha

3 cups 1-inch-cubed pineapple

Cooked white rice, for serving

Thinly sliced scallion, for garnish

Preheat a 5- to 6-quart slow cooker.

Place onions, garlic, and ginger in the slow cooker. Top with short ribs in a tight layer. In a bowl, whisk together brown sugar, soy sauce, vinegar, and hot sauce; pour over ribs.

Cover and cook on high until ribs are almost tender, 4 hours (or on low for 7 to 8 hours). Add pineapple and cook until tender, 1 hour (or on low for 2 hours).

With a slotted spoon, transfer ribs, pineapple, onions, and ginger to a platter and tent with foil. With a ladle, skim fat from cooking liquid. Serve ribs and pineapple mixture with rice, drizzle with some cooking liquid, and top with scallions. (Short ribs and cooking liquid can be refrigerated in an airtight container for up to 3 days.)

Flavored with a heady mixture of cloves, bay leaves, allspice, ginger, and black peppercorns, and braised in a combination of beer and water, this hearty one-pot meat-and-potatoes meal is as tasty as it is fuss-free. Ask your butcher for corned beef or, if you have time, corn it yourself.

New England Boiled Dinner

SERVES 6 TO 8

1 corned beef (about 4 pounds)

6 cups boiling water

1 bottle (12 ounces) dark ale, such as Guinness

¼ teaspoon ground cloves

2 dried bay leaves

2 garlic cloves

½ teaspoon ground allspice

½ teaspoon ground ginger

1 teaspoon yellow mustard seeds

1 teaspoon black peppercorns

1½ pounds small white potatoes, peeled and halved if large

4 carrots, quartered lengthwise

1 small head cabbage, cored and quartered

Prepared horseradish, grainy mustard, and cornichons, for serving

Preheat a 5- to 6-quart slow cooker.

Place corned beef, boiling water, beer, cloves, bay leaves, garlic, allspice, ginger, mustard seeds, and peppercorns in the slow cooker. Cover and cook on low until beef is cooked through, 6 hours (do not cook on high). Add potatoes and carrots, cover, and continue to cook 75 minutes on low. Add cabbage, cover, and cook on low 45 minutes longer.

Remove meat and vegetables from liquid. Slice corned beef against the grain and serve with vegetables, horseradish, mustard, and cornichons.

Corned Beef: In a large stockpot with lid, combine 2 quarts water, 1 cup **coarse salt**, ½ cup packed **brown sugar**, 1 (3-inch) **cinnamon stick**, 2 teaspoons **yellow mustard seeds**, 1 tablespoon **black peppercorns**, 10 **cloves**, 10 **allspice berries**, 3 **dried bay leaves**, and 1 teaspoon **ground ginger**; bring to a boil. Remove from heat and let cool completely. Add 1 first cut of **brisket** (about 4 pounds), trimmed of excess fat, and refrigerate 4 to 5 days. Remove brisket from brine (discard liquid) before proceeding with recipe.

Crushed tomatoes, red wine, and fennel seeds give this tender pork shoulder recipe its decidedly Italian accent. Polenta makes the most natural accompaniment, although pasta and couscous are also good options. Serving it with red wine, however, is (almost) nonnegotiable.

Italian Braised Pork

SERVES 4

2 tablespoons extra-virgin olive oil

2½ pounds boneless pork shoulder

Coarse salt and freshly ground pepper

1 large onion, finely chopped

3 garlic cloves, minced

1 celery stalk, finely chopped

¾ teaspoon fennel seeds

½ cup dry red wine

1 can (28 ounces) crushed tomatoes

Cooked polenta

Finely grated Parmigiano-Reggiano, for serving

Preheat a 5- to 6-quart slow cooker.

In a large skillet, heat oil over medium-high. Season pork with salt and pepper. Cook, turning occasionally, until browned on all sides, about 8 minutes. Transfer pork to the slow cooker.

Reduce heat to medium; add onion, garlic, celery, and fennel seeds to skillet; cook until onion is softened, about 4 minutes. Add wine. Cook, scraping up browned bits with a wooden spoon, until reduced by half, about 2 minutes. Add to slow cooker along with tomatoes. Cover and cook on high until pork is very tender, 4 hours (or on low for 8 hours).

Transfer pork to a cutting board. Using two forks, shred meat into bite-size pieces, discarding any large pieces of fat. Skim fat off sauce. Return shredded pork to slow cooker and stir to combine. Serve over polenta, sprinkled with cheese.

Hominy, the key ingredient in this Southwestern stew, is made from corn. The process involves boiling the dried kernels in water treated with slaked lime; once the kernels swell, the hulls and germs are removed. We use canned hominy in our posole, for convenience; if you can't find it, feel free to swap in white or kidney beans.

Pork Posole

SERVES 6

2 tablespoons vegetable oil

1¼ pounds boneless pork shoulder, trimmed and cut into 4-inch pieces

Coarse salt

1 white onion, chopped, plus more for serving

4 garlic cloves, minced

2 tablespoons chili powder

4 cups low-sodium chicken broth, store-bought or homemade (page 256)

2 cans (15 ounces each) hominy, drained and rinsed

Chopped avocado, sliced radishes, fried tortilla strips or corn chips, and lime wedges, for serving

Preheat a 5- to 6-quart slow cooker.

Heat 1 tablespoon oil in a large skillet over medium-high. Season pork with salt. Add pork to skillet and cook until pieces are browned on all sides, about 8 minutes. Transfer to the slow cooker.

Heat remaining tablespoon oil in skillet. Add onion, garlic, and chili powder, and sauté until soft, 4 minutes. Add 2 cups broth and cook, stirring and scraping up browned bits with a wooden spoon. Transfer to slow cooker. Add remaining 2 cups broth to slow cooker. Cover and cook on high until meat is very tender, 4 hours (or on low for 8 hours).

Using two forks, shred pork. Return to stew and stir in hominy. Stir to heat through, and season to taste with salt. Serve with avocado, radishes, tortilla strips, and lime.

Every Italian family boasts its own take on ciambotta, and each dish is one of a kind. The component they all share is meltingly tender vegetables. This recipe features fresh green beans, tomatoes, potatoes, and sweet Italian sausages. Serve it with garlic bread and olive oil, for drizzling.

Sausage and Vegetable Ciambotta

SERVES 6

1 tablespoon extra-virgin olive oil, plus more for serving

1 pound sweet Italian sausage, casings removed

1 small onion, finely chopped

4 garlic cloves, thinly sliced

2 large tomatoes, cored and chopped

1½ teaspoons chopped fresh rosemary

2 tablespoons tomato paste

2 cups low-sodium chicken broth, store-bought or homemade (page 256)

1 pound fingerling potatoes, scrubbed and cut into ½-inch pieces

½ pound green beans, cut into 2-inch lengths

Coarse salt and freshly ground pepper

2 tablespoons chopped fresh basil, plus whole leaves, for garnish

Preheat a 5- to 6-quart slow cooker.

In a large skillet, heat oil over high. Add sausage and cook, separating meat with the back of a wooden spoon, until no longer pink, about 6 minutes. Stir in onion and garlic, and cook until softened and lightly browned, about 8 minutes. Stir in tomatoes and rosemary, and cook until softened, 2 to 3 minutes. Add tomato paste and broth, and bring to a boil.

Transfer skillet mixture to the slow cooker; add potatoes and green beans, and season with salt and pepper. Cover and cook on high until thick and tender, about 4 hours (or on low for 8 hours). Stir in chopped basil, top with whole leaves, and serve with olive oil, for drizzling.

Tip
Put foods that require more cooking (like potatoes) near the bottom and sides of the slow cooker insert, where heat is concentrated.

Think of this crowd-pleasing, very versatile roast the next time you have friends coming over. Just be sure to season the pork shoulder in advance (at least six hours or, ideally, a day ahead). Serve it sliced, with salsa verde and raw vegetables (like the tiny ripe tomatoes pictured), with roasted potatoes and garlicky greens, or in sandwiches on focaccia or ciabatta.

Porchetta

SERVES 8

2 tablespoons whole fennel seeds

1 to 2 tablespoons red-pepper flakes, to taste

¼ cup fresh thyme leaves

¼ cup fresh rosemary, chopped

2 teaspoons coarsely chopped fresh sage leaves

3 garlic cloves, chopped

Finely grated zest of 1 lemon

1 tablespoon coarse salt

1 teaspoon freshly ground black pepper

¼ cup extra-virgin olive oil

1 (5-pound) boneless pork-shoulder roast, skin removed, cut into 2 equal pieces

Tip

Porchetta is traditionally made with fennel pollen, which is harvested from fennel flowers at the peak of bloom; it has a sweeter and more intense flavor than fennel seed. If you can find it (available from many online sources, including Kalustyan's), by all means use it.

In a small skillet over medium heat, toast fennel seeds and red-pepper flakes until fragrant, about 1 minute. Transfer to a food processor. Add thyme, rosemary, sage, garlic, lemon zest, salt, and black pepper. Add 3 tablespoons oil and pulse until mixture forms a paste.

Spread paste all over pork, dividing evenly; tie each with kitchen twine at 2-inch intervals. Tightly wrap pork in plastic wrap or in a resealable plastic bag and place in a bowl. Refrigerate at least 6 hours or up to overnight, turning occasionally. Before cooking, bring roast to room temperature (about 2 hours).

Preheat a 5- to 6-quart slow cooker.

Heat remaining tablespoon oil in a Dutch oven or other large heavy-bottomed pot. Brown both pieces of pork on all sides, about 15 minutes.

Transfer pork to the slow cooker. Cover and cook on low until an instant-read thermometer inserted into thickest part of each roast registers 180°F to 190°F, about 4 hours (or on high for 2 hours). Transfer roasts to a cutting board. Tent with foil and let rest 30 minutes before slicing. Pour meat juices into a heatproof measuring cup and allow fat to separate, about 5 minutes; skim off fat. Serve jus alongside sliced pork.

Guanciale is a cured meat similar to pancetta or bacon. Here, as in many Italian dishes, just a little bit of it goes a long way toward adding big flavor (in this case, to a bowl of long-simmered chickpeas). With some toasted bread on the side and a bottle of extra-virgin oil, this is *cucina povera* at its most elemental—simple, satisfying, and utterly delicious.

Chickpeas with Guanciale

SERVES 4 TO 6

1 pound dried chickpeas, picked over and rinsed

2 ounces guanciale or pancetta, diced

1 onion, finely chopped

2 small carrots, finely chopped

1 celery stalk, finely chopped

6 garlic cloves

6 thyme sprigs

2 dried bay leaves

¼ cup extra-virgin olive oil, plus more for drizzling

6 to 7 cups boiling water

Coarse salt and freshly ground pepper

Chopped fresh herbs, such as flat-leaf parsley, basil, or mint, for garnish

Toasted bread, for serving

Place chickpeas in a large bowl; cover with water by several inches. Refrigerate, covered, overnight; drain. (To quick soak, cover chickpeas with water in a large saucepan. Bring to a boil. Remove from heat. Let stand, covered, for 1 hour; drain.)

Preheat a 5- to 6-quart slow cooker.

In a small skillet over medium heat, cook guanciale until crisp and fat is rendered, stirring occasionally, about 10 to 15 minutes. Transfer to the slow cooker.

Add onion, carrots, and celery to skillet, and cook until onions are just softened, about 5 minutes. Transfer to slow cooker. Pierce garlic cloves with a fork or hold with tongs and char directly over a flame until softened. Add charred garlic, thyme, bay leaves, olive oil, and chickpeas to slow cooker. Pour in the boiling water, enough to cover. Cook on low until chickpeas are tender, 8 hours (or on high for 4 hours). Add 2 teaspoons salt and cook on low 15 minutes more. Discard bay leaves before serving. Season with salt and pepper. Top chickpeas with chopped herbs, and serve with toasted bread.

Making the celebrated meat sauce of Bologna is not all that different from making a stew, so the recipe transitions easily from the stovetop to the slow cooker. Nevertheless, because there's less evaporation in the machine, you may want to thicken the sauce a bit before tossing with pasta. If so, simmer it in a large saucepan for about 10 minutes.

Spaghetti Bolognese

SERVES 4

- 3 tablespoons extra-virgin olive oil
- 3 onions, finely chopped
- 2 garlic cloves, minced
- 4 carrots, finely chopped
- 3 celery stalks, finely chopped
- 2 tablespoons fresh thyme leaves
- 1½ pounds ground beef, such as chuck or sirloin
- 1 pound ground pork
- 2 cans (14.5 ounces each) diced tomatoes
- 1 cup dry red wine
- ½ cup milk

  Coarse salt and freshly ground pepper

- 1 pound spaghetti, cooked, for serving

  Chopped fresh flat-leaf parsley, for serving

  Finely grated Parmigiano-Reggiano, for serving

Preheat a 5- to 6-quart slow cooker.

Heat olive oil in a large skillet over medium-high. Add onions and cook until soft and translucent, about 6 minutes. Add garlic and cook 1 to 2 minutes more. Add carrots, celery, and thyme and cook until just beginning to soften, about 5 minutes; transfer mixture to the slow cooker.

Return skillet to heat. Add beef and pork; cook over medium heat, stirring frequently and separating meat with the back of a wooden spoon, until cooked through, about 5 minutes. Add tomatoes, wine, milk, 1½ teaspoons salt, and ¼ teaspoon pepper; stir to combine.

Transfer mixture to slow cooker, cover, and cook on high until thickened, about 3 hours (or on low for 6 hours). Serve over spaghetti with chopped parsley and grated cheese.

Orange marmalade and red-wine vinegar combine to give this dish a tanginess that's the perfect complement to rich pork shoulder. Try serving peppery greens (we like watercress) or fresh herbs on the side. Refrigerate any leftover pork in the sauce, to keep it moist.

Marmalade and Vinegar Pork

SERVES 8

4½ pounds pork shoulder, excess fat trimmed, cut into 2-inch pieces

Coarse salt

1 teaspoon fennel seeds, toasted

½ teaspoon red-pepper flakes

¾ cup orange marmalade

¼ cup red-wine vinegar

1 rosemary sprig

4 garlic cloves, smashed and peeled

Flaky salt, such as Maldon, for serving

1 small orange, cut into wedges, for serving

Preheat a 5- to 6-quart slow cooker.

Very generously season pork with coarse salt. Place in the slow cooker.

In a small bowl, mix fennel seeds, red-pepper flakes, marmalade, vinegar, rosemary, and garlic; pour over pork. Cover and cook on low until meat is pull-apart tender, about 8 hours (or on high for 4 hours).

Using a slotted spoon, transfer pork to a large bowl. Strain sauce through a fine sieve, discarding solids. Skim fat from surface of sauce. Spoon pork into serving bowl. Top with flaky salt, and serve with orange wedges.

Here's a good reason to bring the slow cooker along on your summer vacation. Throwing the ribs into the machine (after an overnight soak in a few bottles of beer), then letting them braise all day, allows you plenty of time for recreation—or rest and relaxation. You just need to quickly finish the ribs in the oven to allow the sticky glaze to caramelize a bit. Serve with your favorite potato salad, coleslaw, and fresh summer produce.

Beer-Braised Pork Ribs

SERVES 4 TO 6

FOR BARBECUE SAUCE

- 2 tablespoons extra-virgin olive oil
- 2 onions, finely chopped
- 1 garlic clove, minced
- 1 can (15 ounces) tomato puree
- 1 cup beer
- ¼ cup molasses
- 1 tablespoon Dijon mustard
- 1 tablespoon brown sugar
- 1 tablespoon Worcestershire sauce
- Coarse salt and freshly ground pepper

FOR RIBS

- 3 bottles (12 ounces) beer, preferably pale ale
- 5 pounds baby-back pork ribs
- 2 onions, sliced
- 2 garlic cloves, smashed and peeled
- 3 dried bay leaves
- 2 teaspoons salt
- Pinch freshly ground pepper
- 1 cup Barbecue Sauce, plus more to taste

Make barbecue sauce: Heat oil in a saucepan on medium. Add onions and garlic, and cook, stirring occasionally, until onions are translucent and golden, 8 minutes. Stir in tomato puree, beer, molasses, mustard, brown sugar, and Worcestershire sauce. Increase heat to medium-high and bring sauce to a boil. Reduce heat to a simmer, stirring occasionally, until sauce reaches slightly sticky consistency, about 45 minutes. Let cool. Season with salt and pepper; puree in a blender until smooth. (Barbecue sauce can be refrigerated, covered, for up to 5 days.)

Make ribs: Pour 2 bottles of beer into a deep roasting pan. Add ribs, cover, and refrigerate at least 4 hours and up to overnight.

Preheat a 6- to 7-quart slow cooker. Transfer ribs to the slow cooker (discard beer marinade). Add onions, garlic, bay leaves, remaining bottle of beer, and enough cold water to just cover ingredients. Add salt and pepper, cover, and cook on low 8 hours (do not cook on high), rotating ribs once or twice during cooking.

Preheat oven to 400°F. Using tongs, transfer ribs to a large rimmed baking sheet; arrange in a single layer. Brush ribs with barbecue sauce to coat, and cook until meat starts to char and sauce begins to caramelize, about 20 minutes.

Pork chops cut from the shoulder have a lot of connective tissue that breaks down as they cook, making them a great choice for low and slow cooking. Browning the slab bacon and pork chops in a pan first helps build layers of flavors for this dish; braised red cabbage, applesauce, and sour cream served alongside give it old-fashioned comfort-food appeal.

German-Style Pork Chops

SERVES 4

½ red cabbage, cored and thinly sliced lengthwise

½ red onion, thinly sliced

⅛ teaspoon ground allspice

4 thyme sprigs

Coarse salt and freshly ground pepper

4 ounces slab bacon, cut into ½-inch pieces

4 pork shoulder chops (¾ inch thick, about 9 ounces each)

1 tablespoon extra-virgin olive oil

1 tablespoon unsalted butter

¾ cup low-sodium chicken broth, store-bought or homemade (page 256)

¼ cup apple cider vinegar

Applesauce and sour cream, for serving

In a large bowl, toss cabbage and onion with allspice and thyme. Season with salt and pepper. Transfer to the slow cooker.

In a large skillet over medium-high heat, cook bacon until it begins to brown and crisp, 5 to 7 minutes. Using a slotted spoon, transfer to a 5- to 6-quart slow cooker.

Season pork chops with salt and pepper. Raise heat to high, and heat oil and butter in skillet. Working in batches if necessary, cook chops, turning once and pressing with tongs to make contact with pan, until deep golden brown on both sides, 8 to 10 minutes total. Transfer to the slow cooker.

Add broth and vinegar to skillet, scraping up any brown bits with a wooden spoon. Pour over chops. Cover and cook on low 3 hours (or on high for 1½ hours). Serve chops and cabbage with applesauce and sour cream.

Equal parts ground cloves, cinnamon, fennel seed, star anise, and Szechuan peppercorns, Chinese five-spice powder lends an irresistible flavor to pork. Don't overlook the chili oil served alongside; it really brings everything (broth, pork, noodles, and vegetables) together beautifully.

Roasted Five-Spice Pork with Udon

SERVES 6

3 pounds bone-in pork shoulder, skin removed

Coarse salt and freshly ground black pepper

2 teaspoons five-spice powder

2 tablespoons canola or safflower oil

1 onion, halved

1 large leek (white and tender green parts only), thinly sliced

2 large garlic cloves, minced

1 (3-inch) piece fresh ginger, peeled and minced

4 cups low-sodium chicken broth, store-bought or homemade (page 256)

½ cup low-sodium soy sauce

½ cup dry sherry

1 star anise

1 small fresh red chile (seeds removed for less heat, if desired)

1 tablespoon dark brown sugar

2 cups sliced shiitake mushrooms

2 large carrots, julienned

12 ounces udon noodles

Thinly sliced scallions and sugar snap peas, and hot chili oil, for serving

Preheat a 5- to 6-quart slow cooker.

Rub pork evenly with salt, black pepper, and five-spice powder. In a large Dutch oven or other heavy-bottomed pot, heat oil over medium-high. Add pork and brown on all sides, about 15 minutes. Transfer to the slow cooker.

Skim off all but 2 tablespoons fat from Dutch oven. Add onion, leek, garlic, and ginger to pot, and sauté 2 minutes. Pour in 1 cup broth, stirring and scraping up any browned bits on bottom of pot with a wooden spoon. Spoon onion mixture over pork in slow cooker. Pour soy sauce, sherry, and remaining 3 cups broth over pork. Add star anise and chile, and sprinkle with brown sugar. Cover and cook on low until pork is fork-tender, about 6 hours. Transfer pork to a cutting board, tent with foil, and let rest for 30 minutes.

Strain broth and return it to slow cooker. Add mushrooms and carrots, cover, and cook on low 30 minutes.

Cook udon until al dente. Drain; rinse briefly under cold water and drain again.

Using two forks, pull pork apart into bite-size pieces. Divide udon among 6 bowls. Add pork, then ladle broth and vegetables over noodles. Top with scallions and sugar snaps, and drizzle with chili oil before serving.

There are as many recipes for pulled pork as there are devoted fans (in other words, too many to count). This one is among our favorites for a few reasons: The list of ingredients is short, as is the number of steps, and it delivers delicious results without a lot of effort. That means big returns on very little, almost marginal, investment.

Pulled Pork

SERVES 8

1 onion, finely chopped

1 teaspoon dried oregano

2 dried bay leaves

1 chipotle chile in adobo sauce, minced, plus 1 tablespoon sauce

1 can (28 ounces) crushed tomatoes

1 can (14.5 ounces) whole tomatoes in puree

2 teaspoons coarse salt

½ teaspoon freshly ground pepper

2¾ pounds boneless pork shoulder, trimmed and halved crosswise

Preheat a 5- to 6-quart slow cooker.

Combine onion, oregano, bay leaves, chipotle and sauce, crushed and whole tomatoes (with puree), salt, and pepper in the slow cooker. Add pork and turn to coat completely. Cover and cook on high until meat is pull-apart tender, about 6 hours (or on low for 12 hours).

Transfer pork to a bowl and shred with two forks. Return pork to slow cooker and toss with sauce. Discard bay leaves.

Tip

We like this pork served sandwich-style in soft white rolls with coleslaw and pickles, but also wrapped in warm tortillas, over rice or other grains, and on top of cheese nachos with all the usual fixings.

Layered with meat sauce, no-boil noodles, and shredded mozzarella, this pasta casserole has "potluck" written all over it. The meat sauce cooks quickly on the stovetop, but hours in the slow cooker deepen the flavor. Don't be tempted to use fresh mozzarella; supermarket varieties work better for this recipe. Serve the lasagna with a simple green salad.

Sausage Lasagna

SERVES 8

1 pound Italian pork sausage, casings removed

1 pound ground beef sirloin

1 onion, finely chopped

2 carrots, finely chopped

2 garlic cloves, minced

Coarse salt and freshly ground pepper

1 can (6 ounces) tomato paste

1 can (28 ounces) crushed tomatoes in puree

9 no-boil lasagna noodles

2 cups coarsely grated part-skim mozzarella (8 ounces)

Preheat a 5- to 6-quart slow cooker.

In a 5-quart Dutch oven or heavy pot, cook sausage and beef over medium-high, breaking up meat with a spoon, until no longer pink, 4 to 6 minutes. Add onion, carrots, and garlic; season with salt and pepper. Cook until onion has softened, about 5 minutes. Stir in tomato paste, then tomatoes; bring to a boil, and remove from heat.

Spoon 2 cups meat sauce into the slow cooker. Layer 3 noodles (breaking them as needed to fit), 2 cups meat sauce, and ½ cup cheese; repeat with two more layers (refrigerate ½ cup cheese for topping). Cover and cook on low, 4 to 6 hours (or on high for 2 to 3 hours).

Top lasagna with reserved cheese. Cover and cook on low until cheese has melted, about 10 minutes, before serving.

This French classic takes homey pork and beans to another level with the addition of duck confit (available at many specialty stores and easy enough to make yourself, see page 123). Not quite the labor of love of traditional cassoulet, which can take up to four days, this one still requires a *little* effort, but the payoff is worth it.

Cassoulet

SERVES 10

- 1 pound dried cannellini beans, picked over, rinsed, and soaked (see quick-soaking method on page 207)
- 1 boneless pork shoulder, with skin (1¾ pounds)

  Coarse salt and freshly ground pepper
- ¼ cup duck fat or extra-virgin olive oil
- 2 large shallots, minced
- 4 garlic cloves, smashed and peeled
- 1 tomato, finely chopped
- 4 cups chicken broth, store-bought or homemade (page 256)
- 2 dried bay leaves
- 6 thyme sprigs, tied with kitchen string
- 1 cup plain panko
- 3 duck confit legs, skinned and boned (for recipe, see page 123)
- 12 ounces andouille sausage, sliced into ¼-inch rounds

Tip
Don't worry if the pork shoulder you use is skinless; the skin from the duck confit can work, too. There's no need to add it to the slow cooker since it's already cooked—just broil it at the end.

Add beans to a 5- to 6-quart slow cooker.

Using a sharp knife, remove skin from pork, and cut out a 6-inch square (discard the rest). Trim fat from skin square to ½ inch. Cut pork into 16 squares; season with salt and pepper.

In a large, heavy skillet, heat 2 tablespoons duck fat over high. Cook pork pieces until browned all over, 10 to 12 minutes. Using a slotted spoon, transfer to the slow cooker. Add shallots and garlic to skillet; cook, stirring, until golden, about 5 minutes. Add tomato; cook 2 minutes. Add broth, bay leaves, and thyme, and bring to a simmer; pour into slow cooker. Lay pork skin on top, nestling it into the liquid. Cover and cook on high until pork and beans are tender, 3½ hours. Transfer pork skin to a cutting board.

Wipe out skillet and heat remaining 2 tablespoons duck fat on high. Add panko and cook, stirring, until golden. Stir ¼ cup toasted panko into slow cooker; reserve the rest. Add duck and sausage. Cover and cook on high 1 hour longer. Remove bay and thyme bundle.

Preheat broiler. Line a rimmed baking sheet with foil; place pork skin on pan. Broil on center rack of oven, turning occasionally, until skin is brown and crisp, 10 to 12 minutes. Transfer to cutting board and cut into pieces. Serve cassoulet topped with pork skin and reserved panko.

We like to serve these succulent ribs with soba noodles tossed with scallions, plus a light dressing of safflower oil, toasted sesame oil, lime juice, and rice vinegar. Shred any leftover meat to serve on buns with an Asian slaw of shredded carrots and red cabbage.

Vietnamese Baby Back Ribs

SERVES 4 TO 6

2   shallots, finely chopped

¼   cup Vietnamese fish sauce, such as *nuoc nam*

¼   cup honey

Coarse salt and freshly ground pepper

1   rack spareribs (about 4 pounds), cut into 3 pieces

Preheat a 5- to 6-quart slow cooker.

Stir together shallots, fish sauce, honey, 1½ teaspoons salt, and ½ teaspoon pepper in the slow cooker. Add spareribs and toss to coat. Cook on low until tender and beginning to fall off the bone, 7 hours (we found these cook better on low), turning ribs halfway through.

Preheat oven to broil, with rack 4 inches from heating element. Transfer ribs to a rimmed baking sheet, meat side up. Broil until browned, about 4 minutes.

Pour juices from slow cooker through a fine sieve into a small saucepan (discard solids). Bring to a boil, then cook until syrupy, 5 to 10 minutes. Brush some glaze onto ribs. Serve ribs with remaining glaze.

We love this slow-cooker version of split-pea soup, from our friend and colleague chef Emeril Lagasse. It's packed with vegetables, some healthy fiber, and a good dose of protein. And the best part? Putting it all together is as easy as it gets. It's a great option for weeknights or weekends.

Split Pea with Ham Soup

SERVES 10

10 cups low-sodium chicken broth, store-bought or homemade (page 256)

2 pounds dried green split peas, picked over and rinsed

1 onion, diced

4 small carrots, chopped

1 celery stalk, chopped

½ red bell pepper, chopped

4 garlic cloves, minced

1 tablespoon minced fresh thyme leaves (or 1 teaspoon dried thyme, crumbled)

2 dried bay leaves

2 small ham hocks (1¼ pounds total), with several ½-inch slits cut into skin

Coarse salt and freshly ground pepper

Crusty bread, for serving

In a pot, bring broth to a boil; carefully pour into a 5- to 6-quart slow cooker. Add split peas, onion, carrots, celery, bell pepper, garlic, thyme, bay leaves, and ham hocks. Season with salt and pepper. Cover and cook on high, stirring occasionally, until split peas are creamy, 6 hours (or on low for 12 hours).

Remove ham hocks from cooker. Discard skin and bones; dice meat. Discard bay leaves. Lightly mash peas with the back of a wooden spoon. Add diced ham to soup and season with salt and pepper. Serve with crusty bread.

Choucroute garnie, the famed Alsatian dish of sauerkraut (*choucroute*), potatoes, and a variety of smoked, cured meats, is quintessential cold-weather comfort food. Serve it with an assortment of breads, mustards, and beer or Riesling wine. Using Porkette, a smoked boneless pork butt, is one supermarket shortcut we can really get behind.

Choucroute Garnie

SERVES 8

1½ teaspoons juniper berries

1 teaspoon black peppercorns

1½ teaspoons coriander seeds

1½ teaspoons caraway seeds

2 dried bay leaves

6 thyme sprigs

1 pound slab bacon, cut into 1-inch pieces

1½ pounds smoked pork shoulder butt, peeled and cut into 3 chunks

4 fully cooked bratwurst (about 14 ounces)

3 andouille sausage (10 to 12 ounces)

½ cup dry Riesling wine

¼ cup duck fat or extra-virgin olive oil

2 large onions, thinly sliced

1 large tart green apple, such as Granny Smith, peeled, cored, and finely chopped

2 pounds sauerkraut, drained, rinsed, and squeezed dry

2 cups low-sodium chicken broth, store-bought or homemade (page 256)

Boiled small potatoes (about 2 pounds), for serving

Preheat a 5- to 6-quart slow cooker. Bundle juniper berries, peppercorns, coriander, caraway seeds, bay leaves, and thyme in a square of cheesecloth. Tie with twine and transfer to the slow cooker.

In a large skillet over medium-high heat, cook bacon until crisp, about 8 minutes. Using a slotted spoon, transfer bacon to slow cooker, leaving fat in skillet. Cook pork shoulder in skillet until browned all over, about 8 minutes; add to slow cooker. Cook bratwurst and andouille until browned, about 5 minutes. Transfer sausages to a plate. Add Riesling and cook, stirring and scraping up any browned bits, until reduced by half, about 2 minutes. Transfer to slow cooker.

Wipe out skillet and heat duck fat on high. Cook onions and apple until softened and just beginning to brown, about 10 minutes. Stir in sauerkraut; cook until dry, about 5 minutes more. Transfer to slow cooker with broth. Nestle sausages so they're partly submerged in broth. Cover and cook on high for 3½ hours (or on low for 7 hours).

Transfer meats and sauerkraut (discard spice bundle) to a deep platter; surround with potatoes. Slice pork butt. Strain pan juices into a heatproof measuring cup and spoon off fat. Pour liquid over meats and serve.

Here a whole lamb shoulder is braised in the slow cooker until it's silky and supple and easy to shred. A few aromatics give it distinctive flavor, among them saffron and dried lime, available at Middle Eastern markets and from online grocers. Serve the lamb over red or white quinoa, and garnish with pomegranate seeds, pistachios, and chopped fresh dill.

Persian Lamb Stew

SERVES 6 TO 8

1 lamb shoulder (4 to 5 pounds)

Coarse salt and freshly ground pepper

2 tablespoons extra-virgin olive oil

2 large onions, finely chopped

2 large carrots, finely chopped

2 celery stalks, finely chopped

1 teaspoon dried dill weed

1 head garlic, cloves peeled

3 thyme sprigs

1 cup dry white wine

1 cup fresh orange juice

1 dried lime

1 large pinch saffron threads

Cooked quinoa, for serving

Coarsely chopped fresh dill, pomegranate seeds, and unsalted pistachios, for garnish

Preheat a 5- to 6-quart slow cooker.

Season lamb with salt and pepper. In a large Dutch oven, heat oil over medium-high. Add lamb and cook until golden brown all over, about 8 minutes. Transfer to the slow cooker.

Add onions, carrots, celery, and dill weed to Dutch oven and cook, stirring often, until vegetables are tender, 6 to 8 minutes. Transfer to slow cooker. Add garlic, thyme, wine, orange juice, dried lime, and saffron. Cover and cook on low, until meat is falling apart and shreds easily, 7 to 8 hours (or on high for 5 to 6 hours). Skim fat from surface. Serve stew over quinoa, topped with dill, pomegranate seeds, and pistachios.

This Mediterranean-style one-pot dish is perfect for Easter, or for any Sunday dinner. Lamb shanks are at their best when gently cooked, and here they spend several hours in the slow cooker with a few highly flavorful aromatics and vegetables. Ask your butcher to cut and trim the shanks.

Lamb with Olives and Potatoes

SERVES 4

1¼ pounds small white potatoes,
   scrubbed and halved or quartered
   if large

4 large shallots,
   cut into ½-inch wedges

3 garlic cloves, minced

1 tablespoon finely grated lemon zest,
   plus 2 tablespoons fresh lemon juice

3 rosemary sprigs

   Coarse salt and freshly
   ground pepper

¼ cup all-purpose flour

¾ cup low-sodium chicken broth,
   store-bought or homemade
   (page 256)

3½ pounds lamb shanks,
   cut crosswise into 1½-inch pieces
   and trimmed of excess fat

2 tablespoons extra-virgin olive oil

½ cup dry white wine

1 cup pitted green olives, halved

   Crusty bread, for serving

Combine potatoes, shallots, garlic, lemon zest, and rosemary in a 5- to 6-quart slow cooker; season with salt and pepper. In a small bowl, whisk together 1 tablespoon flour and the broth. Add to slow cooker.

Place remaining 3 tablespoons flour on a plate. Season lamb with salt and pepper, then coat in flour, shaking off excess. In a large skillet, heat oil over medium-high. In batches, cook lamb until browned on all sides, about 10 minutes; transfer to slow cooker.

Add wine to skillet and cook, scraping up any browned bits with a wooden spoon, until reduced by half, about 2 minutes. Add to slow cooker, then cover and cook on low until lamb is tender, about 7 hours (or on high for 3½ hours). Stir in olives, cover, and cook on high for 20 minutes more (or on low for 40 minutes).

Transfer lamb and vegetables to a platter. Skim fat from cooking liquid, then stir in lemon juice and season with salt and pepper. Serve lamb and vegetables with sauce and bread.

Poultry

Coq au Vin,
page 115

The Basics

It can be confounding how little it takes for chicken and turkey to dry out as they cook. The good news, however, is that using the slow cooker can help you avoid this pitfall—especially when you choose the right cuts. Whole chickens, legs and thighs, and turkey wings work best, because they hold up well to hours of gentle heat. The rich fats from the skin or the dark meat maintain moisture as they enhance the flavor of whatever dish they're featured in, and bones enrich the cooking liquid, often eliminating the need to add store-bought broth to the pot.

When using the slow cooker, think of fat as your friend. Remember to play to the strength of the machine, as well as the ingredients you're adding. Case in point: In testing, we didn't have much luck with boneless, skinless chicken breasts—that weeknight dinner staple— because the tough, dried-out results simply were not worth waiting around for (they're also the most expensive cuts of chicken you'll find in any supermarket). So you won't find any recipes for boneless breasts in this book.

On the other hand, dishes that might seem too messy or ambitious in their conventional cooking methods end up making perfect sense in the slow cooker. Duck Confit—a French bistro classic that involves slowly poaching the duck meat in its own fat—feels completely approachable for the home cook when prepared in the slow cooker. When making duck carnitas, the meat falls off the bone in succulent, tender chunks, and then turns deliciously crisp in minutes in a hot skillet with the drippings from the crock. Wrapped in a warm corn tortilla with some sliced avocado and red onion, it will redefine your idea of homemade tacos.

You might never assume from looking at it, but your slow cooker can be your passport to the best of global cooking, especially when preparing poultry. Every culture, it seems, has its own version of an irresistible dish featuring a braised or stewed bird—whether it's Indian Chicken Curry, the Singaporean favorite Hainanese Chicken, Ethiopian Chicken Stew, or Thai chicken soup, Tom Kha Gai. Julia Child may have had to go all the way to the Cordon Bleu in Paris to learn how to make a perfect Coq au Vin. To make ours, you'll just need to put your slow cooker to work.

Recipes

Chicken Chili Tacos

Chicken Thighs with Cilantro Chutney

Spicy Buffalo Chicken Sandwiches

Tom Kha Gai

Chicken Curry

Chicken with 20 Cloves of Garlic

Chicken Tagine

Tex-Mex Chicken and Beans

Chicken Mole

Chicken Korma

Coq au Vin

Hainanese Chicken

Ethiopian Chicken Stew

Turkey Chili

Duck Confit

Duck Carnitas Tacos

Duck with Sour Cherries and Port

Duck Ragù

For this memorable, truly fix-it-and-forget-it chicken dish, use a high-quality store-bought salsa to save time without skimping on flavor; be sure to choose a jar with a short ingredient list. Serve them in corn or flour tortillas, or hard corn taco shells—whichever you prefer.

Chicken Chili Tacos

SERVES 4

2 pounds boneless, skinless chicken thighs (about 6)

4 garlic cloves, thinly sliced

½ cup mild or medium salsa, plus more for serving

1 to 2 tablespoons chopped chipotle chiles in adobo sauce

1 tablespoon chili powder

Coarse salt and freshly ground pepper

8 taco shells or tortillas

Grated cheddar cheese, sour cream, chopped avocado, fresh cilantro, and lime wedges, for serving

Preheat a 5- to 6-quart slow cooker.

Combine chicken, garlic, salsa, chiles, chili powder, 1 teaspoon salt, and ¼ teaspoon pepper in the slow cooker. Cover and cook on high until chicken is cooked through, 4 hours (or on low for 8 hours).

Transfer chicken to a bowl. Using two forks, shred chicken; moisten with cooking liquid. Season with salt and pepper. Serve in taco shells, with cheese, sour cream, avocado, cilantro, lime wedges, and salsa.

Two techniques keep things interesting in this super-easy slow-cooked supper: Chopped onions are browned on the stovetop first, to add complexity to the chicken as it cooks, and a quick homemade chutney is stirred in toward the end, to keep the flavors bright.

Chicken Thighs with Cilantro Chutney

SERVES 4 TO 6

2 tablespoons extra-virgin olive oil

2 onions, coarsely chopped

2½ pounds boneless, skinless chicken thighs, cut into 1½-inch pieces

Coarse salt and freshly ground pepper

1 tablespoon minced peeled fresh ginger

5 garlic cloves, thinly sliced

1 jalapeño chile (ribs and seeds removed for less heat, if desired), thinly sliced, plus more for serving

4 cups packed fresh cilantro, plus more for garnish

½ cup roasted peanuts, plus more, chopped, for serving

2 teaspoons light brown sugar

1 tablespoon fresh lime juice, plus wedges for serving

Preheat a 5- to 6-quart slow cooker.

Heat a large skillet over medium-high. Add oil and onions; cook, stirring occasionally, until browned, about 8 minutes. Transfer to the slow cooker.

Season chicken with salt and pepper; add to slow cooker along with ginger, garlic, and jalapeño. Cover and cook on high until chicken is tender, 2 hours (or on low for 4 hours).

In a food processor, pulse cilantro, peanuts, brown sugar, and lime juice just until finely chopped (do not process to a paste); transfer to slow cooker. Cover and continue to cook on high 30 minutes (or on low for 1 hour). Season with salt and pepper. Serve with jalapeño, cilantro, peanuts, and lime wedges.

Many slow-cooker recipes with similar names simply call for a bottle of barbecue sauce tossed with chicken pieces. This recipe teaches you how easy it is to develop much better, fresher-tasting barbecue flavor from scratch, with just a few pantry staples.

Spicy Buffalo Chicken Sandwiches

SERVES 8

1 tablespoon extra-virgin olive oil

2 pounds boneless, skinless chicken thighs, cut into 1½-inch pieces

Coarse salt and freshly ground pepper

1 onion, finely chopped

3 garlic cloves, chopped

1 red bell pepper, finely chopped

¼ cup water

1 can (14.5 ounces) crushed tomatoes

¼ cup hot-pepper sauce

3 tablespoons Worcestershire sauce

2 tablespoons yellow mustard

1 tablespoon unsulfured molasses

8 hamburger buns, for serving

Pickled vegetables, for serving

Preheat a 5- to 6-quart slow cooker.

In a large skillet, heat oil over medium-high. Add half the chicken, and season with salt and pepper. Cook, stirring once, until meat is golden brown, about 5 minutes. With a slotted spoon, transfer to the slow cooker, leaving as much oil behind as possible. Repeat with remaining chicken.

Reduce heat to medium. Add onion, garlic, bell pepper, and the water to skillet. Cook, stirring and scraping up any browned bits from bottom with a spoon, until onion is translucent, about 5 minutes. Season with salt and pepper. Transfer to the slow cooker and toss with chicken.

Add crushed tomatoes, hot-pepper sauce, Worcestershire, mustard, and molasses to slow cooker; stir to combine. Cover and cook on high until chicken is very tender, 4 hours (or on low for 8 hours).

Transfer chicken to a large plate. Using two forks, shred chicken; return to sauce. Season with salt and pepper. Serve on buns, with pickled vegetables on the side.

While this soup can be made on the stovetop in under an hour, it benefits from a longer spell in the slow cooker. The lemongrass and lime leaves infuse more flavor into the broth and the tender, moist chicken thighs.

Tom Kha Gai

SERVES 6

3 lemongrass stalks, tough outer layers removed

3 cups low-sodium chicken broth, store-bought or homemade (page 256)

¼ cup fish sauce

1 tablespoon sugar

1 (2-inch) piece fresh galangal or ginger, peeled and thinly sliced

6 kaffir lime leaves, halved, or 6 strips lime zest with a vegetable peeler

1 shallot, thinly sliced

3 Thai bird chiles

1½ pounds boneless, skinless chicken thighs, cut into ½-inch strips

4 ounces shiitake mushrooms, stemmed, thinly sliced

1 can (13.5 ounces) unsweetened coconut milk

1 large carrot, finely chopped

3 tablespoons fresh lime juice

¼ cup chopped fresh cilantro, plus more for garnish

2 tablespoons chopped Thai basil, plus more leaves for garnish

1 scallion, thinly sliced

Chili oil sauce, for serving

Preheat a 4-quart slow cooker.

On a cutting board, using the side of a chef's knife, lightly smash lemongrass. Combine lemongrass, broth, fish sauce, sugar, galangal, lime leaves, shallot, chiles, chicken, and mushrooms in the slow cooker. Cover and cook on high until chicken is cooked through, about 2½ hours (or on low for 5 hours).

Add coconut milk and carrot, and cook on high 30 minutes longer (or on low for 1 hour). Stir in lime juice, cilantro, basil, and scallion. Top with cilantro and basil, and serve with chili oil sauce.

Tip

Chili oil sauce—a mixture of ground dried chiles, soybean oil, garlic, and sesame oil—is sold in Asian markets and even many supermarkets. It can be used in any recipe that calls for red-pepper flakes.

It takes only ten minutes of prep work for this creamy coconut curry; the rest happens in the slow cooker. While it cooks, assemble all the accompaniments: basmati rice, naan, assorted pickles and chutneys, and a few vegetables (we like stir-fried cabbage with mustard seeds and green beans).

Chicken Curry

SERVES 8

3 pounds boneless, skinless chicken thighs

2 onions, halved and thinly sliced

8 garlic cloves, thinly sliced

1 (2-inch) piece peeled fresh ginger, thinly sliced

2 tablespoons curry powder, preferably Madras

1 teaspoon ground coriander

1 teaspoon ground cumin

2 teaspoons coarse salt

2 cups unsweetened coconut milk

2 packages (10 ounces each) frozen green peas

Cooked basmati rice, for serving

Preheat a 5- to 6-quart slow cooker.

Place chicken, onions, garlic, ginger, curry powder, coriander, and cumin in the slow cooker, and toss to coat. Add salt. Cover and cook on high until chicken is fork-tender, about 4 hours (or on low for 8 hours).

Stir in coconut milk and peas. Cover and cook on high until peas are heated through, about 20 minutes (or on low for 40 minutes).

Transfer chicken to a bowl. Using two forks, break chicken into pieces. Return chicken to pot and toss with sauce. Serve with rice and desired accompaniments.

Developing this recipe—a riff on the French bistro classic—taught us a thing or two about how the slow, steady, moist heat of the slow cooker really intensifies flavors. When we tried the traditional 40-clove recipe, the garlic flavor was so strong, we cut the number in half (and we love garlic!).

Chicken with 20 Cloves of Garlic

SERVES 6 TO 8

8 whole chicken legs (about 4 pounds)

1 teaspoon extra-virgin olive oil

Coarse salt and freshly ground pepper

20 garlic cloves

2 lemons, thinly sliced

6 thyme sprigs

Crusty bread, for serving

Preheat a 5- to 6-quart slow cooker; preheat oven to broil.

Place chicken skin side up on a rimmed baking sheet. Rub oil onto skin and season generously with salt and pepper. Broil until skin is brown in places. Transfer chicken to the slow cooker. Add garlic, lemons, and thyme. Cover and cook on high until meat is tender and cooked through, about 2½ hours (or on low for 5 hours). Serve with braised garlic, cooking liquid, and bread.

This Moroccan dish is named for its cooking vessel—a shallow clay pot with a tall cone-shaped lid. As the food cooks, steam rises into the lid and the condensation drips back in, much like with the slow cooker. This tagine includes expected ingredients—preserved lemon, green olives, and apricots—and surprises like kaffir lime leaves. While not traditional, they bring a wonderful, heady aroma to the stew.

Chicken Tagine

SERVES 4

1 teaspoon ground cumin

½ teaspoon paprika

¼ teaspoon cayenne pepper

1 teaspoon dried oregano

Coarse salt and freshly ground black pepper

8 bone-in, skin-on chicken thighs (about 3 pounds)

2 tablespoons extra-virgin olive oil

3 onions, finely chopped

4 garlic cloves, mashed to a paste

¾ cup dried apricots, thinly sliced

1 preserved lemon, finely chopped

3 kaffir lime leaves

1 cup green olives, pitted

1 cup boiling water

1 cup dry white wine

Cooked couscous, harissa, and fresh mint, for serving

Preheat a 5- to 6-quart slow cooker.

Combine cumin, paprika, cayenne, oregano, 1 teaspoon salt, and ¼ teaspoon black pepper in a bowl. Rub chicken with spice mixture, coating evenly.

Heat oil in a Dutch oven or other large heavy-bottomed pot over medium. Add chicken, skin side down, and sear until golden brown, about 4 minutes. (Thighs should release naturally from pan when done.) Transfer to the slow cooker.

Add onions and garlic to Dutch oven, and cook until onions are tender, about 6 minutes. Transfer to slow cooker. Add apricots, preserved lemon, lime leaves, olives, the boiling water, and wine to slow cooker. Cover and cook on high 2 hours (or on low for 4 hours). Season with salt and pepper, garnish with mint, and serve with harissa and couscous.

Tip

To make garlic paste: Chop garlic cloves and add a large pinch of coarse salt. Mash into a paste with the flat side of a chef's knife, moving the knife back and forth as you mash.

Here, beans are used to bulk up a simple Southwestern stew to help a little bit of chicken go a long way. Since we skipped the step of browning the meat first on the stovetop, we opted for skinless pieces; the skin doesn't take on any caramelization in the slow cooker, and the resulting texture could compromise the appeal of your finished dish.

Tex-Mex Chicken and Beans

SERVES 4

1 cup dried pinto beans, rinsed

1 jar (11 ounces) mild or medium salsa (1½ cups)

2 tablespoons chopped chipotle chile in adobo sauce

2 tablespoons all-purpose flour

1 cup water

1½ pounds boneless, skinless chicken thighs (about 8)

Coarse salt and freshly ground pepper

1 red onion, chopped

1 red bell pepper, chopped

Sour cream, finely chopped jalapeño, hot sauce, and tortilla strips or chips, for serving

Place beans in a large bowl; cover with water by several inches. Refrigerate, covered, overnight; drain. (To quick soak, cover beans in a large saucepan with water. Bring to a boil. Remove from heat. Let stand, covered, for 1 hour; drain.)

Preheat a 5- to 6-quart slow cooker.

Place beans, salsa, chiles, flour, and the water in the slow cooker; stir to combine. Season chicken with salt and pepper; arrange on top of bean mixture. Scatter onion and bell pepper on top of chicken. Cover and cook on low for 8 hours (or on high for 4 hours).

Transfer chicken from slow cooker to a large plate. Using two forks, shred chicken into large pieces; return to stew. Serve with sour cream, jalapeño, hot sauce, and tortilla strips.

It takes hours for the flavors of authentic mole—smoky chiles, almonds, pepitas, raisins, sweet spices, and chocolate—to meld, so it's tailor-made for the slow cooker. We cooked chicken thighs in this mole rojo, for tacos. Try leftover sauce with fried eggs or rice, or in enchiladas.

Chicken Mole

SERVES 6 TO 8

12 bone-in, skinless chicken thighs (5 pounds), trimmed of excess fat

Coarse salt and freshly ground pepper

¼ cup canola or safflower oil

3 dried ancho chiles

2 dried guajillo chiles

2 ounces bittersweet chocolate, chopped

1 chipotle chile in adobo sauce

1 can (14.5 ounces) whole or diced tomatoes with their juices

1 onion, coarsely chopped

2 large garlic cloves

⅓ cup roasted almonds

⅓ cup pepitas, toasted, plus more for serving

¼ cup raisins

½ teaspoon dried oregano

¼ teaspoon dried thyme

1 teaspoon ground coriander

¼ teaspoon ground cinnamon

⅛ teaspoon ground cloves

1½ cups low-sodium chicken broth, plus more if needed

Warm tortillas, lime wedges, sliced red onion, and cilantro, for serving

Preheat a 5- to 6-quart slow cooker.

Season chicken with salt and pepper. In a large nonstick skillet, heat 1 tablespoon oil over high. Working in batches, cook chicken, turning occasionally, until browned, about 8 minutes; transfer to the slow cooker.

Meanwhile, stem and seed dried chiles, and place in a bowl. Cover chiles with boiling water. Let stand until softened, 15 to 20 minutes. Drain; transfer chiles to a blender. Add chocolate, chipotle, tomatoes, onion, garlic, almonds, pepitas, raisins, oregano, thyme, coriander, cinnamon, cloves, broth, 1 tablespoon salt, and remaining 3 tablespoons oil; puree until smooth. Pour over chicken and stir to combine. Cover and cook on high until chicken is tender, about 3½ hours (or on low for 7 hours).

Transfer chicken to a platter. Pull meat from bones in large pieces. Thin sauce with additional broth, if needed. Serve with tortillas, lime, onion, cilantro, and pepitas.

Tip
If the chiles are dried out or too hard to work with, hold them over an open flame (with tongs) until pliable, about 10 seconds.

Creamy, fragrant, and rich, this curry exemplifies the classic Mughlai cuisine of northern India and Pakistan. It gets its silkiness from cream, yogurt, and ground nuts. As a shortcut in this recipe, we use store-bought almond and cashew butters instead of grinding our own.

Chicken Korma

SERVES 6 TO 8

2	tablespoons unsalted butter
2	large onions, thinly sliced, plus more for garnish
6	cardamom pods
1	tablespoon garam masala
¾	teaspoon ground turmeric
½	teaspoon cayenne pepper
3	pounds boneless, skinless chicken thighs, cut into 2-inch pieces
¼	cup cashew butter
¼	cup almond butter
½	cup plain yogurt
½	cup heavy cream
1	tablespoon tomato paste
2	tablespoons grated peeled fresh ginger
2	garlic cloves
1½	tablespoons sugar
2	teaspoons coarse salt
	Cooked white rice and cilantro sprigs, for serving

Preheat a 5- to 6-quart slow cooker.

In a large skillet, melt butter over medium-high heat. Add onions; cook, stirring occasionally, until golden, 10 minutes. Stir in cardamom pods, garam masala, turmeric, and cayenne; cook until fragrant, 2 minutes. Transfer spices to the slow cooker. Add chicken to slow cooker and toss with spice mixture.

In a blender, combine cashew butter, almond butter, yogurt, cream, tomato paste, ginger, garlic, sugar, and salt; puree until smooth. Pour into slow cooker and stir well to combine. Cover and cook on high until chicken is tender, 3½ hours (or on low for 7 hours). Remove and discard cardamom pods. Serve chicken korma with rice, topped with cilantro sprigs and sliced onions.

Tip

Don't have nut butters? Just add a scant ½ cup each roasted cashews and almonds to the blender. The sauce may not be as smooth, but it will be just as delicious.

The ultimate dinner party dish, coq au vin is named for the wine that mellows into a velvety sauce, punctuated by smoky bacon and earthy mushrooms. We've added carrots, onion wedges, and chopped garlic to the mix. It needs little more than crusty bread and salted butter served alongside, although mashed potatoes or egg noodles are also quite nice.

Coq au Vin

SERVES 6 TO 8

12 bone-in, skin-on chicken thighs (about 5 pounds)

Coarse salt and freshly ground pepper

¼ cup all-purpose flour

6 slices bacon, coarsely chopped

¼ cup extra-virgin olive oil

16 ounces white mushrooms, quartered

3 garlic cloves, chopped

3 small onions, cut into large wedges

9 small carrots, halved lengthwise

¾ cup boiling water

1½ cups dry red wine

4 thyme sprigs

Preheat a 5- to 6-quart slow cooker.

Season chicken with salt and pepper, then toss with flour to coat thighs, shaking off excess. In a skillet, cook bacon over medium heat until edges are crisp, around 15 minutes. With a slotted spoon, transfer bacon to a paper-towel-lined plate and let drain. Reserve fat in pan.

Add mushrooms and garlic to pan, and cook over medium heat until golden brown, about 8 minutes. Transfer to the slow cooker. Add 2 tablespoons olive oil, the onions, and carrots to pan. Increase heat to medium-high and cook vegetables until browned, about 5 minutes. Transfer to slow cooker.

Add remaining 2 tablespoons oil to pan. In two batches, add chicken thighs and cook until browned all over, about 8 minutes per batch. With a slotted spoon, transfer to slow cooker. Pour off excess fat and return pan to heat. Add wine, scraping up brown bits from the bottom. Bring wine to a boil, then reduce heat and simmer 5 minutes. Pour wine and the water over chicken. Sprinkle with bacon and thyme. Cover and cook on low until chicken is tender, 5 to 6 hours (or on high for 2½ hours). Remove chicken and vegetables from sauce and skim any fat. Season with salt and pepper, and serve.

Named for the island of Hainan, off the southern coast of China, this comfort-food classic involves gently poaching a chicken in a flavorful broth, which doubles as the cooking liquid for rice. The national dish of Singapore, it's also increasingly popular in the United States.

Hainanese Chicken

SERVES 6

FOR CHICKEN AND BROTH

- 2 bunches whole scallions, trimmed
- 1 bunch cilantro
- 1 whole chicken (about 4 pounds)
- 4 fresh or dried Asian chiles
- 4 whole star anise
- 8 (¼-inch) slices peeled fresh ginger
- 2 garlic cloves
- 1 teaspoon peppercorns, preferably white
- 8 cups boiling water
- ½ cup low-sodium soy sauce
- 2 tablespoons fish sauce, such as *nam pla* or *nuoc nam*

FOR RICE

- 1 garlic clove, minced
- 1½ teaspoons finely grated peeled fresh ginger
- 1½ cups jasmine rice

  Hot chili oil, for serving

Tip

It's traditional to use the rendered fat from the broth to sauté the aromatics for the rice, so don't discard it!

Preheat a 5- to 6-quart slow cooker.

Make chicken and broth: Place scallions (reserving 2) and half the cilantro in the slow cooker. Top with chicken. Arrange chiles, star anise, ginger, garlic, and peppercorns around chicken. Add the boiling water, soy sauce, and fish sauce (liquid will not cover chicken). Cover and cook on high until chicken is cooked through and an instant-read thermometer inserted into thickest part of a thigh registers 165°F, about 3 hours (or on low for 6 hours). Transfer chicken to a cutting board and cover loosely with foil.

Make rice: Strain broth (you should have about 8 cups; reserve 2½ cups and set aside remainder for another use). Skim fat from surface of broth and add about 2 tablespoons fat to saucepan. Add garlic and ginger; cook on high heat until fragrant, about 1 minute. Add rice and stir to coat. Add reserved 2½ cups broth and bring to a boil. Cover and simmer on low until liquid is absorbed, about 17 minutes. Let stand 5 minutes, then fluff with a fork.

Carve chicken into portions and slice. Thinly slice reserved scallions; chop remaining cilantro. Divide chicken and rice among plates; top with chopped cilantro and scallions. Serve with broth, and drizzle with chili oil.

This fragrant stew, known as *doro wat,* may be the most traditional (and well-known) Ethiopian dish. It relies on berbere—a blend of spices that includes ginger, cardamom, coriander, nutmeg, cloves, cinnamon, and allspice—for its distinctive, inimitable flavor. Look for it at specialty grocers; otherwise, you can find the blend (or recipes for it) online. Serve with black lentils, injera (Ethiopian flatbread), and plain yogurt.

Ethiopian Chicken Stew

SERVES 4

8 bone-in, skin-on chicken thighs (about 3 pounds)

¼ cup berbere (Ethiopian spice blend)

Coarse salt and freshly ground pepper

2 tablespoons Niter Kibbeh (spiced clarified butter; page 267)

3 onions, halved and thinly sliced

6 garlic cloves, minced to a paste

1 (2-inch) piece fresh ginger, peeled and grated

1 can (28 ounces) whole tomatoes

1 (3-inch) cinnamon stick

3 cardamom pods, crushed

1 cup low-sodium chicken broth, store-bought or homemade (page 256)

Preheat a 5- to 6-quart slow cooker.

Coat chicken evenly with berbere, 1 teaspoon salt, and ¼ teaspoon pepper. Heat Niter Kibbeh in a large heavy-bottomed skillet over medium-high. Working in batches if necessary, arrange thighs, skin side down, in skillet (do not crowd). Sear until golden, 8 to 10 minutes, reducing heat to medium if chicken begins to brown too quickly. Turn chicken and brown other side, about 5 minutes. Transfer to the slow cooker.

Add onions, garlic, and ginger to skillet; cook over low heat until very soft and golden, about 10 minutes. Transfer to slow cooker. Chop tomatoes and add (with their juices). Add cinnamon, cardamom, and broth. Cover and cook on low until chicken is tender and stew has thickened slightly, 4 hours (or on high for 2 hours). Season generously with salt and pepper, and serve.

Making turkey chili in the slow cooker is nothing new. Yet this recipe relies on a few tricks to make it as robust as any beefy chili you'd find over a cowboy's campfire. It gets deep flavor from a smoky ancho-tomato puree, and hearty texture from shredded smoked turkey wings.

Turkey Chili

SERVES 8

3 ounces dried ancho chiles (about 5), stemmed and seeded

Boiling water, for chiles

Coarse salt and freshly ground pepper

¼ cup safflower or canola oil

2 pounds ground dark turkey meat

½ large white onion, diced

3 garlic cloves, minced

½ teaspoon ground cinnamon

1 teaspoon dried oregano

1 teaspoon ground cumin

1 can (28 ounces) whole fire-roasted tomatoes, coarsely chopped (reserve 1 cup juice)

½ cup low-sodium chicken broth, store-bought or homemade (page 256)

1 can pinto beans (15.5 ounces), rinsed and drained

¾ pound smoked turkey wings, skin removed

Cooked rice, sliced jalapeño chiles, grated cheddar cheese, and sliced red onion, for serving

Preheat a 5- to 6-quart slow cooker.

Place chiles in a bowl and cover with boiling water. Let stand until softened, 15 to 20 minutes. Transfer chiles and ¼ cup soaking liquid to a blender, add a pinch of salt, and puree to a smooth paste.

Heat 2 tablespoons oil in a large skillet over medium-high. Add turkey and cook just until no longer pink, 5 to 6 minutes. Using a slotted spoon, transfer turkey to a bowl.

Wipe skillet clean. Heat remaining 2 tablespoons oil over medium. Add onion and cook until soft, about 5 minutes. Add garlic and cook 1 minute more. Stir in cinnamon, oregano, and cumin; cook until fragrant, about 2 minutes. Add chile paste and reserved 1 cup tomato juice, stirring to combine; cook 2 minutes.

Return turkey to skillet. Add broth, season with salt and pepper, and stir well to combine. Bring to a simmer, then transfer mixture to the slow cooker. Stir in chopped tomatoes and beans, and nestle turkey wings in center of slow cooker. Cover and cook on low, 6 to 7 hours (or on high for 3 to 3½ hours).

Remove turkey wings from slow cooker; transfer to a cutting board. Remove meat from bones and shred; transfer to slow cooker and stir. Season with salt and pepper. Serve with rice, jalapeño, cheddar, and red onion.

It's doubtful that the inventor of the slow cooker had confit in mind, but it's another delightful surprise that we discovered in testing. The machine's low setting allows the duck legs to gently poach in the fat for several hours. We like to serve the legs over soft lettuces, with toasted croutons and a grainy-mustard vinaigrette. The meat is also delicious shredded and tossed with pasta, or as a topping for flatbread pizza.

Duck Confit

SERVES 6

- ¼ cup plus 2 tablespoons coarse salt
- 4 large garlic cloves, smashed and peeled
- 4 dried bay leaves, crumbled
- 1 tablespoon juniper berries, crushed
- 1 tablespoon fresh thyme leaves
- 1 teaspoon freshly ground pepper
- 6 duck legs (3½ to 4 pounds), untrimmed
- 6 cups duck fat, olive oil, or lard, or any combination of the three

Tip

Rendered duck fat is a bonus that comes from cooking duck. This recipe yields about 1 cup. Save every drop—it's great for frying potatoes, brushing onto hot grilled bread, and stirring into polenta. (It's also a crucial ingredient in cassoulet; see page 76.) And it keeps in the freezer indefinitely in an airtight container. You can also purchase duck fat. It's occasionally available at specialty stores and butcher shops, and always online.

In a bowl, combine salt, garlic, bay leaves, juniper berries, thyme, and pepper, rubbing spice mixture between your fingers to release aromatic oils. Generously rub onto duck legs, coating evenly. Sandwich legs in pairs, skin side out, tucking in any remaining spice mixture; cover bowl and refrigerate at least overnight or up to 2 days.

Preheat a 5- to 6-quart slow cooker.

Scrape off spice mixture and rinse duck under cold water. Pat completely dry and place in the slow cooker.

In a small saucepan over medium heat, melt duck fat and pour over duck. Cover and cook on low until oil is clear and meat is tender, 6 hours (or on high for 3 hours). Let duck cool completely in fat at room temperature, then refrigerate until ready to serve. Wipe off fat and roast at 425°F just until skin is crisp and duck is heated through. (Reserve duck fat for another use.)

This recipe was inspired by the unbelievably delicious duck tacos served at the restaurant Cosme in New York City. Though the slow cooker works wonders for helping the duck reach falling-off-the-bone perfection, it doesn't get hot enough to sizzle the meat for the trademark carnitas finish. For that, you'll need a skillet and some rendered duck fat (a broiler and a rimmed baking sheet would work, too).

Duck Carnitas Tacos

SERVES 6 TO 8

½ cup fresh tangerine juice (or orange juice)

2 tablespoons fresh lime juice, plus lime wedges for serving

2 chipotle chiles in adobo sauce, finely chopped

2 garlic cloves, minced

1½ teaspoons coarse salt

6 duck legs (3½ to 4 pounds)

Warm tortillas, chopped avocado, chopped radishes, toasted pepitas, and cilantro, for serving

Preheat a 5- to 6-quart slow cooker.

Place tangerine juice, lime juice, chipotles, garlic, and salt in the slow cooker, and stir until combined. Add duck, skin side up; cover, and cook on low until tender, 6 hours (or on high for 3 hours).

Transfer duck to a platter and let cool slightly. Remove skin; pull meat from bones in large pieces. Pour juices into a heatproof bowl; skim off fat into a separate bowl.

In a large nonstick skillet, heat ¼ cup reserved duck fat on high. Add duck and cook, stirring, until crisp, 6 to 7 minutes. Stir a few tablespoons of reserved juices into skillet. Serve immediately with tortillas, avocado, radishes, pepitas, and cilantro.

Duck and cherries make a wonderful pairing. Here, the duck turns delightfully tender in the slow cooker, while the cherries flavor the sauce. (You could also try quartered dried figs in place of the cherries.) Serve this over a bed of wild rice for an authentically all-American matchup.

Duck with Sour Cherries and Port

SERVES 6

6 duck legs (3½ to 4 pounds), excess skin trimmed

Coarse salt and freshly ground pepper

2 tablespoons all-purpose flour, plus more for dusting

1 tablespoon extra-virgin olive oil

8 small shallots, halved

4 thyme sprigs

1 bay leaf

½ teaspoon juniper berries (optional)

½ cup ruby port

1½ cups low-sodium chicken broth, store-bought or homemade (page 256)

⅔ cup dried cherries

3 tablespoons water

Preheat a 5- to 6-quart slow cooker.

Season duck with salt and pepper; dust lightly with flour, shaking off excess. Heat oil in a large nonstick skillet on high. Working in batches, cook duck until browned all over, 7 to 8 minutes. Transfer duck to a platter and skim off all but 1 tablespoon fat. (Reserve remaining fat for another use.)

Add shallots to skillet; cook on medium until lightly browned, 2 minutes. Remove from heat, and add thyme, bay leaf, juniper berries (if using), and port, stirring and scraping up any browned bits with a wooden spoon. Add broth and bring to a boil. Pour into the slow cooker. Nestle duck legs into liquid, cover, and cook on high about 2½ hours (or on low for 5 hours).

Stir in cherries, cover, and cook on high until duck is cooked through, 1 hour longer (or on low for 2 hours). Transfer duck to an aluminum-foil-lined baking sheet, skin side up. Preheat broiler.

Pour cooking liquid into a bowl; skim off fat into a separate bowl (discard juniper berries and bay leaf). Transfer liquid (about 2 cups) to a saucepan and bring to a boil. In a bowl, stir flour with the water until well combined; whisk into boiling broth. Simmer, stirring occasionally, until thickened, 5 minutes.

Broil duck until skin is golden and crisp, about 5 minutes. Serve with sauce.

Think of this as a nice alternative to Bolognese sauce. It's simple enough for a family meal but also an unexpected (in a good way) choice for company. In other words, it's comfort food, but elevated. Serve over wide pappardelle noodles, with the same wine that flavors the ragù.

Duck Ragù

SERVES 8

4 duck legs (about 2½ pounds), skin removed

Coarse salt and freshly ground pepper

2 tablespoons extra-virgin olive oil

2 small onions, diced

2 garlic cloves, thinly sliced

6 ounces baby bella mushrooms, trimmed and chopped

2 carrots, diced

2 celery stalks, diced

1 cup dry red wine

1 cup low-sodium chicken broth, store-bought or homemade (page 256)

1 can (28 ounces) crushed tomatoes

1 dried bay leaf

3 thyme sprigs

1 pound pappardelle, cooked, for serving

Preheat a 5- to 6-quart slow cooker.

Season duck with 1 teaspoon salt and ¼ teaspoon pepper. Heat oil in a large skillet over medium-high. Add duck legs and cook until browned all over, about 7 to 8 minutes. Transfer to the slow cooker.

Add onions to skillet and cook over medium-high until soft and translucent, about 6 minutes. Add garlic, mushrooms, carrots, and celery, and cook until soft, another 5 minutes. Transfer vegetables to slow cooker. Pour wine and broth into skillet, and bring liquid to a boil, stirring and scraping up browned bits with a wooden spoon. Pour into slow cooker.

Stir in tomatoes (with their juices), bay leaf, and thyme. Cover and cook on high until meat is very tender and falling off the bone, about 4 hours (or on low for 8 hours). Pull meat from bones. Return meat to slow cooker and cook on high for 1 hour. Discard bay leaf and season with salt and pepper. Serve ragù over pappardelle.

Seafood

Spanish-Style
Octopus, page 154

The Basics

Fish cooks best in a moist, steamy environment. Sound like any countertop appliance you know? Indeed, the slow cooker is just the thing to make you fall in love with cooking seafood at home. And there is a lot to love: Seafood is healthful (rich in protein, low in fat) and delicious. But it can also be expensive, which can make preparing it feel a little high-stakes, as if you're just one false move—or an extra 30 seconds on the stove—from a culinary disappointment.

The slow cooker can help maximize flavor and texture while minimizing effort (and, as an added bonus, it won't fill your kitchen with any fishy odors). Of course, you need to start with a fish that's well suited to the machine and won't fall apart while cooking, such as salmon, halibut, cod, tuna, or bass. More delicate options like sole and flounder are not good choices for slow cooking.

Shellfish is a surprisingly good fit, as well: The flavor base for classic Bouillabaisse is built before the cockles and mussels are added partway through cooking, to be joined by fish and shrimp in the final half hour. (Just be sure to keep the lid secure, to create enough heat and build up enough steam for the shells to pop open.) Slow-cooker Shrimp, Chicken, and Andouille Gumbo tastes just as good as it does in traditional Cajun cooking, regardless of the two shortcuts involved: using the machine to cook the shrimp at the end—mild heat is the key to tender shrimp—and making the roux in the microwave.

For the simplest preparation, try poaching salmon for just an hour. Because the slow cooker maintains a steady, low temperature, there's no guesswork to determining doneness, and the results are perfectly tender and moist. It's an ideal dish for entertaining: You just need to add a quick, simple salsa verde. And although you may never have thought to poach tuna in oil yourself, our recipe should change that. Ninety minutes is all it takes for fish that you can enjoy as you would canned tuna, with soft lettuces, boiled potatoes, and olives in a Niçoise salad; tossed with pasta; or tucked into a heavenly pan bagnat sandwich with tomatoes, olives, and more olive oil. With this variety of techniques, ideas, and winning recipes, you may just make cooking fish part of your regular routine after all.

Recipes

Seafood Laksa

Poached Salmon with Salsa Verde

Shrimp, Chicken, and Andouille Gumbo

Halibut with Eggplant and Ginger Relish

Chawanmushi

Oil-Poached Tuna

Salt-Baked Fish and Potatoes

Indian-Style Fish Curry

Bouillabaisse

Spanish-Style Octopus

Making a proper Malaysian laksa involves building layers of flavor: first, a paste, followed by a highly aromatic broth that simmers in the slow cooker. Shrimp, mussels, and white fish cook quickly in the broth.

Seafood Laksa

SERVES 6 TO 8

2 tablespoons virgin coconut oil or extra-virgin olive oil

1 small onion, chopped

4 Thai bird chiles

1 (2-inch) piece fresh ginger, peeled and grated

1 (1-inch) piece fresh turmeric, peeled and grated

1 lemongrass stalk, tough outer leaves discarded, inner bulb chopped

¼ cup fresh cilantro

1 tablespoon tamarind paste

½ teaspoon ground cumin

½ teaspoon paprika

1 teaspoon coarse salt

2 cups unsweetened coconut milk

2 cups boiling water

4 kaffir lime leaves

1 teaspoon fish sauce

1 pound medium shrimp, peeled and deveined (shells rinsed and reserved)

2 pounds small mussels, scrubbed

¾ pound firm fish fillet, such as halibut or cod, cut into 1-inch pieces

8 ounces rice noodles

Lime wedges, cubed firm tofu, sliced scallions, sliced Thai bird chiles, cilantro, and chili oil, for serving

Preheat a 7-quart slow cooker.

Heat oil in a saucepan over medium. Add onion and cook until translucent, about 5 minutes. Add chiles, ginger, turmeric, lemongrass, cilantro, tamarind paste, cumin, paprika, and salt. Cook until fragrant, about 2 more minutes. Remove from heat and let cool. Transfer spice mixture to a food processor and puree to a thick paste.

Combine laksa paste, coconut milk, the boiling water, lime leaves, fish sauce, and shrimp shells in the slow cooker. Cover and cook on low for 2 hours (we prefer this recipe on low).

Strain liquid through a medium sieve into a bowl, pressing down on solids; return broth to slow cooker (discard solids). Add shrimp and mussels, and cook on low 20 minutes. Add fish and cook until shrimp is completely cooked through, fish is firm, and mussels open, about 10 minutes.

Meanwhile, prepare noodles according to package instructions.

To serve, divide noodles among bowls. Add broth and seafood, and top with tofu, scallions, chiles, and cilantro. Serve with lime wedges and chili oil.

The slow cooker's value has as much to do with what it *doesn't* do as with what it does. In the case of fish, that means not overcooking it. It's a comfort to know you can poach a whole fillet without the risk of drying it out.

Poached Salmon with Salsa Verde

SERVES 4 TO 6

1½ cups dry white wine

1½ cups water

1 shallot, halved

2 thyme sprigs

1 large dried bay leaf

1 garlic clove, smashed and peeled

2 inner celery stalks, with leaves

1 carrot

2 lemon slices,
plus wedges for serving

6 black peppercorns

2 pounds skin-on salmon,
preferably wild

Coarse salt and freshly
ground pepper

Salsa Verde

Tip
When cooked, the salmon will be delicate. Line the slow cooker with parchment paper large enough to extend over the top of the pot for easy removal.

Preheat a 5- to 6-quart slow cooker.

Place wine, the water, shallot, thyme, bay leaf, garlic, celery, carrot, lemon, and peppercorns in the slow cooker. Cover and cook on high for 30 minutes (or on low for 1 hour).

Check for pin bones in the salmon by running your fingers over the fillets; remove any stray bones with tweezers. Season salmon with salt and pepper, and transfer to slow cooker with poaching liquid. Cover and cook on low until salmon is opaque and flakes easily with a fork, about 1 hour (we prefer the texture of the fish when cooked on low rather than high). For more well-done salmon, continue checking every 15 minutes until fish reaches desired doneness. (Salmon is well done when an instant-read thermometer placed in the thickest part of the fillet reads 145°F.) Serve warm or at room temperature with Salsa Verde.

Salsa Verde: In a food processor or blender, pulse 2 cups **fresh cilantro** leaves, 1 cup **fresh flat-leaf parsley**, ½ cup **extra-virgin olive oil**, 3 tablespoons **fresh lemon juice**, 1 large **garlic clove**, ½ teaspoon **coarse salt**, and ¼ teaspoon **freshly ground pepper** until smooth. Serve immediately.

Our version of this Cajun favorite relies on a roux for thickening the stew, rather than filé powder, which isn't always so easy to find. Making the roux the traditional way, on the stove, can take forty-five minutes. Using the microwave cuts that active time to around ten minutes. Be sure to have oven mitts and a trivet at the ready, as the bowl can get pretty hot.

Shrimp, Chicken, and Andouille Gumbo

SERVES 12

4 pounds boneless, skinless chicken thighs, cut into 1½-inch pieces

1½ pounds andouille sausage or kielbasa, sliced into ½-inch rounds

1 tablespoon chopped fresh thyme leaves

Coarse salt and freshly ground black pepper

1 large onion, finely chopped

1 large red or green bell pepper, finely chopped

4 celery stalks, finely chopped

3 large garlic cloves, minced

2 dried bay leaves

¼ teaspoon cayenne pepper

1 cup all-purpose flour

¾ cup canola or safflower oil

4 cups low-sodium chicken broth, store-bought or homemade (page 256)

¼ cup tomato paste

1 pound large shrimp, peeled and deveined

Cooked white rice, hot sauce, and pickled okra, for serving

In a 5- to 6-quart slow cooker, combine chicken, sausage, and thyme; season with salt and black pepper. In a large bowl, combine onion, bell pepper, celery, garlic, bay leaves, and cayenne.

In a large microwave-safe bowl or heatproof measuring cup, combine flour and oil; microwave on high for 4 minutes; carefully whisk. Microwave on high for 3 minutes more; whisk. (The roux will look dry and pebbly, but should become runny when whisked.) Microwave on high for 1½ minutes more; whisk. Continue microwaving and whisking at 1-minute intervals until roux is color of dark peanut butter. Immediately add chopped vegetables and microwave on high for 2 minutes.

Transfer vegetable mixture to the slow cooker. In a large pot (or the microwave), heat broth and tomato paste; then transfer to slow cooker and stir to combine. Cover and cook on high for 4 hours (or on low for 8 hours). Skim fat, if desired; discard bay leaves. Stir in shrimp, cover, and cook on high until opaque, about 10 minutes more (or on low for 20 minutes). Serve gumbo with rice, hot sauce, and pickled okra.

Another test kitchen favorite, this savory, slow-cooked relish is so delicious we found ourselves inventing new ways to serve it, beyond as a base for flaky pieces of perfectly poached halibut. Try it with grilled chicken or lamb, or as a starter, with soft cheeses and toasted bread.

Halibut with Eggplant and Ginger Relish

SERVES 4

- 4 medium Japanese eggplants (or 2 large eggplants), cut into ½-inch cubes
- ¼ cup coarse salt
- ¼ cup extra-virgin olive oil
- 2 onions, diced
- 3 garlic cloves, minced
- 1 (1-inch) piece fresh ginger, peeled and finely grated
- 2 kaffir lime leaves
- 1 teaspoon brown sugar
- 1 tablespoon rice vinegar
- ¼ cup fresh lime juice
- 1 cup packed fresh cilantro, finely chopped
- 1 pound halibut, cut into 1-inch pieces
- ½ cup unsweetened flaked coconut, toasted, for garnish

Combine eggplant and salt in a colander set over a bowl; let stand about 1 hour. Rinse well and pat dry.

Preheat a 5- to 6-quart slow cooker.

Heat 2 tablespoons oil in a large skillet over medium. Add onions and sauté until deeply golden, about 15 minutes. Add garlic and ginger, and cook 2 more minutes. Add eggplants and cook just until hot. Transfer vegetables to the slow cooker.

Add remaining 2 tablespoons oil, the lime leaves, brown sugar, vinegar, and lime juice to slow cooker. Cover and cook on low until very soft but not mushy, about 4 hours (or on high for 2 hours).

Stir in cilantro. Nestle fish on top of eggplant mixture and cook on low until cooked through, about 20 minutes (or on high for 10 minutes). Serve relish topped with halibut and sprinkled with toasted coconut.

We were surprised and delighted to learn how well this savory egg custard from Japan (one of Martha's favorite dishes) turned out in the slow cooker. It's a sign of great success to serve chawanmushi without any air bubbles, and we were successful at every turn!

Chawanmushi

SERVES 6

2 (2-inch) squares kombu, rinsed

3 cups water

½ cup bonito flakes

1 tablespoon low-sodium soy sauce

2 teaspoons mirin (rice wine)

Coarse salt

6 large eggs

½ teaspoon toasted sesame oil or canola oil

6 shiitake mushrooms, stemmed and thinly sliced

6 large shrimp, peeled and deveined, cut into ½-inch pieces

2 tablespoons sliced scallions (white part only)

Microgreens or radish sprouts, for garnish

Tip

The custard cups make a nice starter or side dish, but they work as a main course as well, supplemented with a hearty salad and miso soup.

In a saucepan, combine kombu with 2 cups water and simmer 10 minutes (do not boil). Add bonito flakes and simmer 2 minutes longer. Strain stock (known as dashi) into a heatproof bowl. Add soy sauce, mirin, and ¾ teaspoon salt. Let cool.

In a bowl, gently beat eggs (try not to incorporate air). Stir in dashi mixture; then strain through fine-meshed sieve with a fork.

In a small skillet, heat oil over high. Add mushrooms, season with salt, and cook until softened but not browned, about 6 minutes. Divide mushrooms, shrimp, and scallions among six 1-cup custard cups or ramekins. Pour custard into each. Gently tap to bring air bubbles to surface. Using a lit match, hover the flame close to custard's surface to remove air bubbles. Cover each ramekin tightly with plastic wrap.

Preheat a 5- to 6-quart slow cooker. Set 4 canning jar lid rings in the slow cooker. Pour boiling water to reach top of rings. Place half the cups in the slow cooker; stack remaining cups atop first layer, staggering them like bricks. Wrap slow-cooker lid tightly with a clean kitchen towel, gathering ends at top (to absorb condensation).

Cook on high until custard is set, 1½ hours (do not cook on low). Remove ramekins from slow cooker and remove plastic. Serve immediately, topped with microgreens, or chill up to overnight.

Once you poach your own tuna in a blend of seasoned oils, you may never buy a can of albacore again. Use the tuna as you would canned: in salads (we love it with radicchio, sliced oranges, and slivered green olives), flaked and mixed with mayonnaise for sandwiches, and tossed with vinaigrette, white beans, and fennel for an Italian-style antipasto.

Oil-Poached Tuna

SERVES 2

- 2 (1-inch-thick) tuna steaks (1¼ pounds)
- 2 teaspoons coarse salt
- 6 (1-inch) strips orange zest, removed with vegetable peeler
- 4 garlic cloves, smashed and peeled
- 2 dried bay leaves
- 1 serrano chile, halved (seeds and ribs removed for less heat, if desired)
- 1 rosemary sprig
- ¼ cup pitted green olives, smashed
- 2 cups canola, safflower, or extra-virgin olive oil, or any combination of the three

Rub tuna all over with the salt and let sit at room temperature for 30 minutes.

Preheat a 4-quart slow cooker.

Place tuna (do not rinse) in the slow cooker. Add orange zest, garlic, bay leaves, chile, rosemary, olives, and oil. Cover and cook on high until tuna is just firm, 1 hour (flip to check underside). Turn off slow cooker, remove cover, and let tuna sit in oil for 30 minutes.

Transfer tuna to a wide bowl and strain oil through a sieve over tuna; discard solids, but reserve olives, if desired.

Tip

Refrigerate any leftovers in the cooled oil (fully submerged) for up to 1 month. The oil can be reused once more to poach another batch.

It seems counterintuitive that this technique, usually reliant on the dry heat of an oven, would work in the slow cooker. But when we conducted this kitchen experiment, we were thrilled with the results. The key is to begin the potatoes an hour before the fish, to give them a head start, and to seal the fish well in parchment, lest it take on too much salt as it steams.

Salt-Baked Fish and Potatoes

SERVES 4

1 lemon, thinly sliced

½ bunch fresh thyme

½ fennel bulb, cored and thinly sliced

1 small garlic clove, thinly sliced

2 whole branzino (about 2 pounds), scaled, gutted, and cleaned (head left on, if desired)

1 tablespoon extra-virgin olive oil, plus more for drizzling

2 pounds small (1 to 1¼ inches) white potatoes, such as Honey Gold, scrubbed

1 box (3 pounds) kosher salt

Preheat a 7-quart slow cooker.

Divide lemon, thyme, fennel, and garlic between fish, stuffing each cavity.

Cover bottom of the slow cooker with a ½-inch layer of salt. Toss potatoes with oil and arrange over salt layer. Bury potatoes in salt, adding more salt, as necessary, to cover. Cover slow cooker and cook on high for 1 hour.

Wrap fish well in a parchment, tucking ends under, and place on top of potato-salt layer. Sprinkle about 1 cup more salt on top. Cover and cook on high until fish is cooked through, about 3 hours.

Carefully lift parchment package out of slow cooker, brushing off salt layer. Open parchment packet and transfer fish to a serving platter. Arrange potatoes around fish, drizzle fish and potatoes with oil, and top with lemon slices.

Curries take exceptionally well to the slow cooker. The only challenging part, admittedly, is gathering the seasonings together, but all are available in large supermarkets, specialty grocers, and online. After that, it's simply a matter of cooking the curry paste for a couple of hours in the machine, then placing the fish on top to finish for a mere twenty minutes. Serve with rice and a green vegetable (we like sautéed spinach here).

Indian-Style Fish Curry

SERVES 4 TO 6

½ cup flaked unsweetened coconut

2 serrano chiles, sliced (seeds and ribs removed for less heat, if desired)

1 teaspoon coriander seeds

½ onion, coarsely chopped

1 (1-inch) piece fresh turmeric, peeled and coarsely chopped

1 (1-inch) piece fresh ginger, peeled and coarsely chopped

2 garlic cloves, thinly sliced

2 tablespoons tamarind paste

1 teaspoon ground cumin

¼ teaspoon fenugreek seeds

1 tablespoon mild curry powder

Coarse salt

2 cans (13.5 ounces each) unsweetened coconut milk

2 pounds firm white fish fillets, such as cod or halibut, cut into 2- to 3-inch pieces

Fresh cilantro, for garnish

Preheat a 5- to 6-quart slow cooker.

Combine coconut, chiles, coriander seeds, onion, turmeric, ginger, garlic, tamarind, cumin, fenugreek, curry powder, and 1 teaspoon salt in a food processor; puree to form a paste. Transfer paste to a saucepan, add coconut milk, and bring to a boil. Transfer coconut mixture to the slow cooker. Cover and cook on high until slightly thickened, 2 hours (or on low for 4 hours).

Season fish with salt and transfer to slow cooker; submerge fish in curry sauce. Reduce slow cooker to low and cook until fish is flaky but does not fall apart, about 20 minutes. Serve fish curry sprinkled with cilantro.

Saffron, lemon zest, and fennel flavor this Provençal fish stew. True to tradition, it's served with toasted bread and rouille—a bright, garlicky mayonnaise scented with cayenne and more saffron. For convenience, our rouille recipe starts with store-bought mayo.

Bouillabaisse

SERVES 6 TO 8

2 tablespoons extra-virgin olive oil

1 onion, diced

1 fennel bulb, trimmed and cut into thin wedges

3 small carrots, thinly sliced

2 large garlic cloves, thinly sliced

Coarse salt and freshly ground pepper

2 tablespoons tomato paste

½ cup dry white wine

½ teaspoon saffron threads, crumbled

3 strips lemon zest

1 can (28 ounces) diced tomatoes

3 cups fish stock, store-bought or homemade (page 258)

1 pound small white potatoes, scrubbed and halved

1 pound cockles or other small clams, scrubbed

½ pound mussels, scrubbed and beards removed

1½ pounds firm fish fillets, such as cod or halibut, cut into 2-inch pieces

1 pound large shrimp, peeled and deveined

Toasted bread, for serving

Rouille

Preheat a 5- to 6-quart slow cooker.

Heat oil in a large, deep skillet over medium-high. Add onion, fennel, carrots, and garlic. Season with salt and pepper, and cook until vegetables are softened, 5 minutes. Add tomato paste and cook on high 1 minute. Add wine, saffron, and lemon zest, and cook until nearly evaporated, 2 minutes. Add tomatoes (with their juices) and cook until very thick, 7 to 8 minutes. Add stock and bring to a boil. Pour into the slow cooker and add potatoes. Cover and cook on high until potatoes are tender, 2½ hours (this recipe works best on high).

Add cockles and mussels. Cover and cook on high until nearly all are opened, 15 to 30 minutes. Push shellfish to the side and add fish and shrimp, making sure they're submerged. Cover and cook on high until fish flakes and shrimp are pink and curled, about 30 minutes.

Ladle broth and potatoes into deep bowls, and divide seafood evenly. Serve with toasted bread and rouille.

Rouille: Mash 1 **garlic clove** with a pinch **coarse salt**, a pinch **cayenne**, and a pinch **saffron** to a paste with a fork or the flat side of a chef's knife. Whisk garlic paste together with 1 tablespoon **fresh lemon juice**, ⅓ cup **mayonnaise**, and ¼ cup **extra-virgin olive oil** until blended and smooth.

Pulpo gallego is one of the culinary treasures of Spain, specifically of Galicia in the northwest corner. It is quintessential tapas-bar food, along with *patatas bravas* (spicy potatoes), marcona almonds, *membrillo* (quince) paste, manchego cheese, and roasted piquillo peppers. Octopus braises beautifully in the slow cooker; just give it a quick boil beforehand to tenderize, and toss it on the grill afterward to get the proper char.

Spanish-Style Octopus

SERVES 6

2 pounds octopus, cleaned (see tip below)

1 small fennel, trimmed, bulb and fronds coarsely chopped

2 small onions, thickly sliced

1 bunch fresh flat-leaf parsley

1 bunch fresh oregano

2 dried bay leaves

¼ cup plus 2 tablespoons extra-virgin olive oil

Coarse salt

2 garlic cloves, minced

¼ cup capers, drained, rinsed, and coarsely chopped

Juice of 2 lemons (about ⅓ cup)

¼ teaspoon hot smoked paprika

¼ teaspoon sweet smoked paprika

Tip
Look for the smallest octopus available. It should be firm to the touch, smell of the sea, and be bright white underneath, with pretty purple-black tendrils. All parts of the octopus, except for the tough top, are edible.

Preheat a 5- to 6-quart slow cooker.

Bring a large stockpot of water to a boil. Add octopus and boil briefly to tenderize, about 2 minutes. Drain and let cool; then slice octopus into 2-inch pieces.

Place fennel, onions, parsley, oregano, and bay leaves in the slow cooker. Arrange octopus over vegetables. Drizzle with 1 tablespoon oil and ½ teaspoon salt. Cover and cook on low until octopus is tender, 2 hours (or on high for 1 hour).

Heat a grill or grill pan to high. Remove octopus and half the vegetables from slow cooker (discard remaining vegetables and liquid); toss with 1 tablespoon oil and grill until charred, about 6 minutes. Transfer to a bowl.

Meanwhile, gently heat remaining ¼ cup oil in a small skillet. Add garlic and cook until just fragrant, about 2 minutes. Stir in capers and lemon juice. Remove from heat and stir in both paprikas. Pour over octopus, toss, season with salt, and serve.

Meatless

Summer Vegetable
Tian, page 172

The Basics

Making meatless meals a bigger part of your dinner rotation—even dinner just one night a week—has been shown to have measurable benefits on your health, your budget, and the environment. When you prepare dinner in the slow cooker, you get the added benefit of more hands-free cooking time—something everyone can appreciate.

We also appreciate that the slow cooker, despite sometimes being considered a throwback to the 1970s kitchen, can be instrumental in turning out of-the-moment dishes that perfectly reflect how vegetarians and carnivores alike are eating right now. A few cases in point: Lentils and Freekeh with Greens, Spring Vegetable Scafata, and Root Vegetable Confit with Pistachio Pesto.

Of course, the slow cooker is excellent at meatless soups like Pasta e Fagioli, when the low, slow heat turns out perfectly creamy white beans. But think beyond the classics: Use the slow cooker to prepare some of your favorite restaurant dishes at home, like Indian Saag Paneer, with a healthy mix of spinach and kale made smooth with an immersion blender.

Perhaps more than anything else, the slow cooker will surprise you with its ability to produce dishes that seem entirely counterintuitive to countertop preparation. Swapping pearl barley for the usual Arborio rice in risotto means you don't have to stand at the stove, stirring; finishing the dish with Parmigiano-Reggiano and goat cheese imparts plenty of rich, creamy flavor and texture. The pasta in Three-Cheese Macaroni goes into the cooker dry, then gets tossed with both milk and evaporated milk. What emerges is comfort food of the highest—and most irresistible—order. It will be just the latest revelation the slow cooker offers, because if it can turn dry elbow macaroni into something with such a silky, luscious texture, it must be capable of (almost) anything.

Recipes

Lentils and Freekeh with Greens

Barley Risotto with Fresh Mushrooms

Spring Vegetable Scafata

Three-Cheese Macaroni

Saag Paneer

Pasta e Fagioli

Summer Vegetable Tian

Root Vegetable Confit with Pistachio Pesto

Dal Tadka

Ribollita

Harira

Freekeh is a wheat berry with origins in the Middle East. The wheat is harvested while the grains are young and green, then fire-roasted. Finally, the husk is rubbed off (*farik* in Arabic, which gives the grain its name). Here, freekeh pairs with beluga lentils and baby greens for a protein-packed powerhouse.

Lentils and Freekeh with Greens

SERVES 8

8 cups vegetable broth, store-bought or homemade (page 259)

¼ cup extra-virgin olive oil, plus more for serving

2 large onions, chopped

4 celery stalks, chopped

2 large carrots, chopped

¼ teaspoon red-pepper flakes

1 cup black beluga lentils (6 ounces), picked over and rinsed

1 cup whole freekeh (4 ounces), rinsed

Coarse salt and freshly ground black pepper

10 ounces baby greens, such as kale or spinach

Shaved Parmigiano-Reggiano, for serving

Preheat a 5- to 6-quart slow cooker. Heat broth in a saucepan over medium-low.

Heat oil in a skillet over high. Cook onions, celery, carrots, and red-pepper flakes until softened, about 8 minutes. Transfer to the slow cooker. Add lentils and freekeh. Pour in broth, and season with salt and black pepper. Cover and cook on high until lentils and freekeh are tender, about 4 hours (or on low for 8 hours). Stir in greens until wilted. Serve drizzled with oil and topped with shaved cheese.

Tip

As the name suggests, black beluga lentils resemble caviar and can be found in supermarkets, specialty markets, or online. French lentils du puy or Spanish pardina lentils, found in most supermarkets, substitute nicely.

You can find recipes for slow-cooker risotto made with traditional Arborio rice, but we prefer the texture of barley here. It holds up beautifully and doesn't get gummy. Earthy mushrooms flavor the dish the whole way through, while two cheeses and fresh chives round things out at the end.

Barley Risotto with Fresh Mushrooms

SERVES 8

- 7 cups vegetable broth, store-bought or homemade (page 259), or water
- 2 tablespoons extra-virgin olive oil
- 2 tablespoons unsalted butter
- 12 ounces fresh mushrooms, such as cremini, shiitake, or oyster, trimmed and sliced
- 2 shallots, finely chopped
- 1 garlic clove, minced
- Coarse salt and freshly ground pepper
- 1 tablespoon fresh thyme leaves
- 2 cups pearl barley
- 2 ounces fresh goat cheese (about ½ cup), crumbled
- ½ cup grated Parmigiano-Reggiano (2 ounces), plus more, shaved, for serving
- Snipped fresh chives, for garnish

Preheat a 5- to 6-quart slow cooker. Heat 6 cups broth in a saucepan over low.

Meanwhile, heat 1 tablespoon oil and 1 tablespoon butter in a large skillet over medium. Add half the mushrooms and sauté until tender, about 4 minutes; transfer to a bowl. Add remaining tablespoon oil and tablespoon butter, and sauté remaining mushrooms until tender, 4 minutes. Return reserved mushrooms to pan. Add shallots, garlic, 2 teaspoons salt, ¼ teaspoon pepper, and thyme; sauté for 2 minutes. Add barley, stirring to coat well. Increase heat to medium-high, add remaining cup broth, and cook, stirring to combine, until completely absorbed, about 4 minutes.

Transfer barley mixture to the slow cooker. Pour in broth and stir to combine. Cover and cook on high until barley is tender but still firm, 2 to 3 hours (or on low for 5 to 6 hours).

Before serving, stir in both cheeses with a fork until melted. Season with salt and pepper. Serve topped with shaved cheese and chives.

Scafata, Italian for "hull," is the perfect vehicle for fresh vegetables that require shucking: fava beans and fresh peas. Add some asparagus and you've got a nice springtime main course. (If you are lucky enough to find fiddlehead ferns, add a quarter pound of them along with the other vegetables; they are the essence of spring.) Serve bowls of scafata with grilled bread, for heft, and a fried egg on top of each, for a boost of protein.

Spring Vegetable Scafata

SERVES 6

¼ cup extra-virgin olive oil, plus more for serving

2 shallots, thinly sliced

1 garlic clove, minced

1 serrano chile (seeds and rib removed for less heat, if desired), thinly sliced

½ teaspoon chopped fresh rosemary

1 small head escarole, leaves thinly sliced

Coarse salt and freshly ground pepper

¼ cup dry white wine

1 cup shelled fresh peas (from about 1 pound in pods)

1 cup shelled and peeled fresh fava beans (from about 1½ pounds in pods)

2 cups sugar snap peas (about 6 ounces)

½ cup boiling water

1 pound asparagus, trimmed and cut into 1-inch pieces

Grilled bread, fried eggs, and finely grated Parmigiano-Reggiano, for serving

Preheat a 5- to 6-quart slow cooker.

Heat oil in a large skillet over high. Add shallots, garlic, chile, and rosemary, and cook until softened, about 5 minutes. Add escarole in batches, allowing it to wilt before adding more. Season with salt and pepper. Pour in wine and bring to a boil. Transfer to the slow cooker.

Add peas, fava beans, and snap peas. Add the boiling water, cover, and cook on high until vegetables are just tender, about 1 hour (or on low for 2 hours). Add asparagus, cover, and cook on high until tender, about 30 minutes longer (or on low for 1 hour).

Tip

To peel fava beans, blanch them in boiling water for 2 minutes. Drain and rinse with cold water. Use your fingernails to break the skin, then gently squeeze to slip out the beans.

For this streamlined recipe, we didn't want to have to boil the pasta before adding it to the slow cooker. We tried putting all the ingredients in the machine, but the sauce tasted much better when the onion was sautéed first; using evaporated milk eliminated the need to thicken the sauce any further. Finally, we finished the whole thing with a shower of golden toasted breadcrumbs added in the last fifteen minutes of cooking.

Three-Cheese Macaroni

SERVES 6

- 2 tablespoons unsalted butter
- ½ small yellow onion, diced
- 3 cups coarsely grated extra-sharp white cheddar cheese (12 ounces)
- 1 cup coarsely grated Gruyère cheese (4 ounces)
- 12 ounces elbow macaroni
- 2 cups milk
- 2 cans (12 ounces each) evaporated milk
- 1 teaspoon Dijon mustard
- ¼ teaspoon cayenne pepper (optional)
- Coarse salt and freshly ground black pepper
- 1⅔ cups fresh breadcrumbs (see page 267)
- ¼ cup finely grated Parmigiano-Reggiano cheese (1 ounce)

Tip
It's important to seek out the best-quality cheese you can find; it definitely makes all the difference in flavor. If you can't find Gruyère, use an equal amount of Comté, Emmental, or Beaufort.

Melt 1 tablespoon butter in a small skillet over medium-high. Add onion and cook until softened, about 5 minutes. Transfer onion to a 5- to 6-quart slow cooker. Add cheddar, Gruyère, macaroni, both milks, mustard, cayenne (if using), ½ teaspoon salt, and ¼ teaspoon black pepper. Stir until macaroni is well coated and submerged in sauce. Cover and cook on low, 2 to 3 hours (or on high for 1 to 1½ hours).

In a skillet, melt remaining tablespoon butter over medium. Add breadcrumbs and toast, stirring often, until golden brown. Transfer to a bowl and mix in Parmigiano-Reggiano. Season with salt and black pepper.

In last 15 minutes of slow cooking, remove lid from cooker and sprinkle pasta with breadcrumbs. Continue cooking, partially uncovered, until liquid is absorbed and top is golden brown. Season with salt and black pepper, and serve.

A vegetarian staple on any Indian restaurant menu, *saag paneer* (spinach and cheese) is actually quite simple to make at home, especially in the slow cooker. We used a combination of spinach and kale for more body (spinach alone ended up too watery and limp).

Saag Paneer

SERVES 6

1½ pounds fresh spinach, coarsely chopped

8 ounces kale, preferably Lacinato, tough stems trimmed and leaves coarsely chopped

1 large red onion, finely chopped

2 tablespoons minced fresh peeled ginger

3 plum tomatoes, chopped

8 garlic cloves, minced

1 small serrano chile (seeds and rib removed for less heat, if desired), minced

2 tablespoons ground cumin

1 teaspoon ground coriander

½ teaspoon ground turmeric

1½ teaspoons garam masala

Coarse salt and freshly ground pepper

2 tablespoons ghee (clarified butter) or unsalted butter

8 to 12 ounces paneer or queso fresco, cut into ¾-inch cubes

Naan or other flatbread, chutney, plain yogurt, and basmati rice, for serving

Preheat a 5- to 6-quart slow cooker.

Combine spinach and kale, and transfer half to the slow cooker. Top greens with onion, ginger, tomatoes, garlic, chile, cumin, coriander, turmeric, garam masala, and ½ teaspoon pepper. Add remaining greens. Gently press down on ingredients, cover, and cook on high until tender and fragrant, 3 hours (or on low for 4 to 5 hours).

Add ghee and 2 teaspoons salt. Use an immersion blender (or transfer to a blender) and puree to desired consistency. Return puree to slow cooker, and season with salt and pepper.

Add cubed paneer, turn slow cooker off, cover, and let sit for about 10 minutes to gently heat cheese. Serve with naan, chutney, yogurt, and rice.

Tip

You can find paneer at Indian grocers, specialty markets, and online. Or try queso fresco in its place; we loved its flavor and consistency with the greens.

Dried beans emerge from the slow cooker creamy and tender without breaking apart. Using a well-seasoned broth (here we kept it vegetarian, but any broth will do) eliminates the extra step of sautéing a soffrito of celery, carrot, and onions at the outset. Add a Parmigiano-Reggiano rind to the soup as it cooks, for even more flavor.

Pasta e Fagioli

SERVES 8

1 pound dried cannellini beans, sorted and rinsed

10 cups vegetable broth, store-bought or homemade (page 259)

2 dried bay leaves

2 large garlic cloves, minced

1 teaspoon chopped fresh rosemary

1 teaspoon chopped fresh thyme leaves

½ teaspoon red-pepper flakes

Coarse salt and freshly ground black pepper

1 pound small pasta, such as tubettini or small shells

4 tablespoons unsalted butter

½ cup finely grated Pecorino Romano cheese (2 ounces), plus shaved for serving

Fresh thyme, for garnish

Extra-virgin olive oil, for drizzling

Place beans in a large bowl; cover with water by several inches. Refrigerate, covered, overnight; drain. (For a quick soak, cover beans in a large saucepan with water. Bring to a boil. Remove from heat. Let stand, covered, for 1 hour; drain.)

Preheat a 5- to 6-quart slow cooker. Heat broth in a saucepan over medium-low.

Add beans to the slow cooker. Transfer broth, bay leaves, garlic, rosemary, thyme, and red-pepper flakes to slow cooker; season with salt and black pepper. Cover and cook on high until beans are tender, about 4 hours (or on low for 8 hours). Discard bay leaves.

Transfer 2 cups beans to a bowl and coarsely mash with a fork. Return to slow cooker and season with salt. Add pasta, cover, and cook on high until al dente, about 20 minutes (or on low for 35 to 40 minutes). Stir in butter and grated cheese. Season with salt and black pepper. Serve hot, topped with shaved cheese and thyme, and drizzled with oil.

This presentation only looks like you exerted a lot of effort. In reality, it is so much less fussy than ratatouille because you don't have to cook each vegetable separately. The only thing you need to speed up prep time is a V-slicer or mandolin: Slice all the vegetables the same thickness and diameter (about two and a half inches) to promote even cooking.

Summer Vegetable Tian

SERVES 6

1 cup Tomato Sauce

1 zucchini, sliced ⅛ inch thick

3 baby eggplants, sliced ⅛ inch thick

3 firm plum tomatoes, sliced ⅛ inch thick

1 long red bell pepper, sliced ⅛ inch thick

1½ teaspoons chopped fresh thyme leaves

½ cup extra-virgin olive oil

Coarse salt and freshly ground pepper

Preheat a 5- to 6-quart slow cooker. Spread Tomato Sauce in bottom of the slow cooker.

In a large bowl, toss zucchini, eggplants, tomatoes, bell pepper, and thyme with 6 tablespoons oil; season with salt and pepper. Stack slices of zucchini, eggplant, tomato, and pepper in piles, alternating vegetables. Lay stacks of vegetables on their sides in slow cooker, making a tight ring around the edge. Lay more vegetables down center, packing them tightly. Drizzle remaining 2 tablespoons oil on top. Cover and cook on high until tender and bubbling, 3½ hours (or on low for 7 hours).

Tomato Sauce: Heat 1 tablespoon **extra-virgin olive oil,** 1 minced large **garlic clove,** and a pinch of **red-pepper flakes** in a pot over medium, stirring frequently, just until fragrant and sizzling, about 2 minutes. Add 1 can (28 ounces) **whole peeled tomatoes,** chopped, and season with **coarse salt** and **freshly ground black pepper.** Bring to a boil over high heat; then reduce to a rapid simmer and cook, stirring occasionally and mashing tomatoes, until thickened, about 15 minutes. Once cooled, sauce can be refrigerated in an airtight container up to 1 week; reheat over low before serving.

In roughly the time it takes to oven-roast vegetables, you can poach them in fragrant oil in the slow cooker. Serve the silky root vegetables with pesto over quinoa as a lovely main course, as a nice accompaniment to roasted meats, or even as part of a cheese board.

Root Vegetable Confit with Pistachio Pesto

SERVES 4 TO 6

4 small carrots, peeled but with ends left intact

4 small parsnips, peeled

2 beets, peeled and cut into ½-inch wedges

8 cipollini onions

1 fennel bulb, cut into wedges with core intact

2 dried bay leaves

1 teaspoon coriander seeds

3 dried red chiles

4 to 5 cups olive or canola oil

Pistachio Pesto

Tip

To brown the vegetables after poaching, heat a large cast-iron skillet or griddle over high. Add vegetables and cook, tossing, until golden, about 5 minutes.

Preheat a 5- to 6-quart slow cooker.

Combine carrots, parsnips, beets, onions, fennel, bay leaves, coriander seeds, chiles, and oil in the slow cooker. Cover and cook on high until tender, about 2½ hours (or on low for 5 hours). Let cool in oil for 30 minutes, then using a slotted spoon, transfer to a wire rack set over a rimmed baking sheet to drain. (Save the flavorful oil to use in dressings, to sauté or fry with, or of course, to poach another batch of vegetables.)

Serve vegetables with Pistachio Pesto.

Pistachio Pesto: In a mini food processor, pulse ½ cup roasted salted shelled **pistachios**; ½ cup packed **fresh flat-leaf parsley**; 1 small **garlic clove,** smashed and peeled; and ½ cup **extra-virgin olive oil** until finely chopped. Add 2 tablespoons **red-wine vinegar** and 2 tablespoons finely grated **Pecorino Romano cheese,** and pulse to combine. Transfer to a bowl.

Unlike most restaurant dals, this one is substantial enough to serve as a main course. *Tadka*, in Punjabi, means "tempered," a culinary term for adding a sauté of flavorful ingredients to something mild. In this case, ginger, cumin, chiles, curry leaves, and tomatoes are sautéed and added to yellow toor dal and simmered until the flavors meld.

Dal Tadka

SERVES 4

1¼ cups yellow toor dal (split pigeon peas), rinsed and sorted

1½ cups hot water, plus more for dal

Coarse salt

¼ cup canola or safflower oil

1 onion, finely chopped

2 garlic cloves, minced

2 serrano chiles, halved (seeds and ribs removed for less heat, if desired)

1 tablespoon minced fresh peeled ginger

1 tablespoon cumin seeds

1½ teaspoons ground turmeric

24 fresh or dried curry leaves

2 plum tomatoes, cored and chopped

2 tablespoons unsalted butter

Cooked white rice and plain yogurt, for serving

In a saucepan, cover dal with water by 1 inch and bring to a boil on high. Reduce heat and simmer 10 minutes; then cover and let sit 30 minutes.

Preheat a 4-quart slow cooker. Drain dal and transfer to the slow cooker. Add 1½ cups hot water and season with salt; cover and cook on high until just tender, about 4 hours (or on low for 8 hours).

In a large skillet, heat oil on high. Add onion, garlic, chiles, ginger, cumin, turmeric, and curry leaves, and cook until onion is soft, 7 to 8 minutes. Add tomatoes, season with salt, and cook until softened, 4 more minutes. Transfer tomato mixture to slow cooker. Cover and cook on high until dal tadka is very tender, 1 hour (or on low for 2 hours). Add butter and whisk to break up some of the mixture. Serve dal tadka over rice with yogurt.

Tip

Toor dal are readily found in Indian and Middle Eastern markets. While not the same, split yellow peas found in supermarkets make a fine substitution. Curry leaves are available from specialty markets and online; we like kalustyans.com.

Meaning "reboiled" in Italian, this vegetarian soup was developed as a way to make good use of stale bread. It's traditionally prepared one day and reboiled the next. This version, featuring zucchini, fresh cranberry beans, and kale, is delicious on the day it's made and for days thereafter.

Ribollita

SERVES 4

¼ cup plus 2 tablespoons extra-virgin olive oil, plus more for serving

1 onion, finely chopped

3 garlic cloves, minced

½ teaspoon red-pepper flakes

1 bunch kale, preferably Lacinato, stems removed, leaves cut into ½-inch ribbons

2 medium zucchini, quartered lengthwise and sliced ½ inch thick

1 large tomato, finely chopped

1 cup fresh or frozen shelled cranberry beans

1½ cups boiling water

Coarse salt and freshly ground black pepper

2 slices country bread

Finely grated Parmigiano-Reggiano, for serving

Preheat a 4-quart slow cooker.

Heat 2 tablespoons oil in a large skillet over high. Add onion, garlic, and red-pepper flakes, and cook until softened, about 5 minutes. Add kale and cook until just wilted, 5 minutes. Transfer kale mixture to the slow cooker.

In same skillet, heat 1 tablespoon oil over high. Add zucchini and cook until lightly browned, 3 to 4 minutes. Transfer zucchini, tomato, cranberry beans, and the boiling water to slow cooker; season with salt and black pepper. Cover and cook on high until beans are tender, 3 hours (or on low for 6 hours).

In skillet, heat remaining 3 tablespoons oil over medium. Add bread and cook, turning once or twice, until golden and crisp, 5 to 6 minutes. Let cool slightly, then tear into pieces; stir into stew. Cover and cook on high until thick, 1 more hour (or on low for 2 hours). Season with salt and black pepper. Serve ribollita topped with grated cheese and drizzled with olive oil.

Tip
Cavolo nero, with its character-istically green-black leaves, is another name for Lacinato kale, dinosaur kale, or Tuscan kale. If not available, regular kale works fine here.

There are countless versions of harira, the national dish of Morocco (and the traditional fast-breaking meal of the holy month of Ramadan). The soup often includes lamb, or at least lamb broth, and some versions include pasta. Our meatless harira gains protein and substance from three types of legumes—chickpeas, green lentils, and red lentils—and is served with toasted flatbread. You can also top it with plain yogurt.

Harira

SERVES 8

1 cup dried chickpeas, picked over and rinsed

2 tablespoons extra-virgin olive oil

1 large onion, finely chopped

3 garlic cloves, minced

1 tablespoon ground ginger

2 teaspoons ground turmeric

1 teaspoon ground cumin

Coarse salt and freshly ground black pepper

½ teaspoon cayenne pepper

Pinch saffron

1 (3-inch) cinnamon stick

1 can (28 ounces) crushed tomatoes

¼ cup chopped fresh cilantro, plus more for garnish

1 cup French green lentils, picked over and rinsed

1 cup red lentils, picked over and rinsed

8 cups boiling water

Toasted flatbread, for serving

For a quick soak, cover chickpeas in a large saucepan with water. Bring to a boil. Remove from heat. Let stand, covered, for 1 hour; drain.

Preheat a 5- to 6-quart slow cooker.

Heat oil in a large skillet over medium-high. Add onion and cook, stirring occasionally, until softened and slightly golden, about 10 minutes. Add garlic, ginger, turmeric, cumin, 1 teaspoon black pepper, cayenne, saffron, and cinnamon. Cook until fragrant, about 2 minutes. Add tomatoes and chopped cilantro, and bring to a boil. Reduce heat to medium and simmer about 5 minutes.

Transfer tomato mixture to the slow cooker. Add green and red lentils, and chickpeas. Stir in the boiling water and 1 teaspoon salt. Cover and cook on high until legumes are tender, about 2½ hours (or on low for 5 hours). Season with salt and black pepper, top with cilantro, and serve with flatbread.

Side Dishes

Braised Fennel with
Olives and Peppers,
page 199

The Basics

The slow cooker is ideal for side dishes in lots of ways (and not just for the obvious benefit of saving space in the oven or on the stovetop for the main course, or even dessert). Sides can sometimes seem like an afterthought, a last-minute effort to round out a meal—something boiled, seasoned, then tossed. But in the slow cooker, these main-course accompaniments can take on unexpected dimension and complexity of flavors. What might have been blanched green beans with salt and butter can now be slow-cooked Greek-Style Green Beans with Tomato. Rather than the same-old copper pennies, there are Carrots with Lime, Ginger, and Honey. When you slow-cook side dishes, you *have* to get started on them a few hours ahead of the meal so they are first-minute, not last. Having a series of single focuses, rather than juggling main and sides at once, benefits the entire meal: You can set up the machine to prepare a hands-free side dish, and then turn your full attention to the main course.

You'll want to choose sturdy vegetables that are well suited to braising and slow-roasting—things like potatoes, winter squash, carrots, fennel, and cauliflower. Take a hearty cruciferous vegetable like red cabbage, toss it with apples, vinegar, and sugar, expose it to several hours of gentle heat, and you end up with a sweetly sour braised partner for weeknight roast chicken, Sunday pork loin, or even the Thanksgiving turkey. Super-dense sweet potatoes, meanwhile, can simply be buttered, wrapped in parchment, and baked to a creamy texture that pairs perfectly with herbed crème fraîche. You can use a more delicate, faster-cooking vegetable, such as corn, but you'll want to gradually bring out its mellow sweetness in a cheesy custard base.

Never underestimate the appeal of that creamy or cheesy base. Investing a few extra minutes at the start, to make a roux or béchamel, will pay you back in spades as everyone around the dinner table polishes off Gruyère-topped Scalloped Potatoes or creamy cauliflower with two cheeses, lemon zest, and toasted breadcrumbs. Sometimes, the most memorable dishes aren't actually the main course but, rather, the crave-worthy sides.

Recipes

Carrots with Lime, Ginger, and Honey

Braised Leeks

Roasted Sweet Potatoes with Herbed Crème Fraîche

Braised Baby Artichokes

Braised Red Cabbage

Greek-Style Green Beans with Tomato

Corn-Chile Pudding

Smoky Collard Greens with Tofu

Braised Fennel with Olives and Peppers

Cauliflower with Cream Sauce

Scalloped Potatoes

Winter Squash with Shallots and Dates

Cider Baked Beans

Carrots with Lime, Ginger, and Honey

SERVES 6 TO 8

¼ cup extra-virgin olive oil

¼ cup honey

3 pounds carrots, cut into
   1- to 1½-inch pieces on the bias

½ teaspoon coarse salt

   Pinch freshly ground pepper

   Ginger-Lime Butter

Preheat a 5- to 6-quart slow cooker.

Combine oil and honey in the slow cooker. Add carrots, salt, and pepper, and toss to coat well. Cover and cook on low until carrots are fork-tender, 2 hours (or on high for 1 hour).

Using a slotted spoon, transfer carrots to a serving bowl. Slice half Ginger-Lime Butter into ¼-inch-thick disks and place on top of carrots.

Ginger-Lime Butter: In a small food processor, pulse 4 tablespoons room temperature **unsalted butter,** ¾ teaspoon **honey,** 1½ teaspoons finely grated **lime zest** plus 1 teaspoon fresh **lime juice** (from 2 limes), 1½ teaspoons grated peeled **fresh ginger,** ⅛ teaspoon **coarse salt,** ⅛ teaspoon **freshly ground black pepper,** and a pinch of **cayenne** until well combined. Spoon butter onto a sheet of plastic wrap or parchment paper and tightly roll into a log, twisting ends to seal. Refrigerate until firm, at least 1 hour and up to 1 week.

Braised Leeks

SERVES 6 TO 8

4 leeks, split lengthwise and rinsed well

   Coarse salt and freshly ground pepper

4 to 6 thyme sprigs

2 dried bay leaves

6 tablespoons unsalted butter,
   cut into small pieces

2½ cups low-sodium chicken broth,
   store-bought or homemade (page 256)

¼ cup extra-virgin olive oil

   Juice of 1 lemon

Preheat a 5- to 6-quart slow cooker.

Arrange leeks in the slow cooker. Season generously with salt and pepper, scatter with thyme and bay leaves, and dot with butter. Pour in broth. Cover and cook on high until leeks are tender and easily pierced with the tip of a knife, 1 to 1½ hours (or on low for 2½ hours). Discard bay leaves. Drizzle leeks with oil and lemon juice before serving.

The texture of slow-cooked sweet potatoes—soft, creamy, buttery—can't be beat. We like them rubbed with butter and seasonings before roasting, then sliced into rounds and served with herb-flecked crème fraîche. Or, try mashing them and serving the crème fraîche on the side.

Roasted Sweet Potatoes with Herbed Crème Fraîche

SERVES 6 TO 8

- 3 tablespoons unsalted butter, room temperature
- 1 teaspoon onion powder
- 1 teaspoon garlic powder
- 1½ teaspoons dried sage
- Coarse salt and freshly ground pepper
- 6 sweet potatoes, scrubbed and pierced with a fork
- ½ cup crème fraîche
- 1 tablespoon mixed fresh herbs, such as flat-leaf parsley, tarragon, and chives, plus more for garnish
- Finely grated zest of 1 lemon

Preheat a 5- to 6-quart slow cooker.

In a bowl, combine butter, onion powder, garlic powder, sage, 2 teaspoons salt, and ½ teaspoon pepper. Rub sweet potatoes with butter mixture, dividing evenly. Tightly wrap each sweet potato in parchment paper, then aluminum foil; transfer to the slow cooker. Cover and cook on high until tender when pierced with a knife, 3 to 3½ hours (or on low for 6 to 7); larger potatoes will take longer to cook.

Combine crème fraîche, mixed herbs, and lemon zest in a small bowl. Season with salt and pepper. Spread herbed crème fraîche on a serving platter, and top with sliced potatoes and more herbs.

The sight of artichokes at the farmers' market is a reason to celebrate the arrival of spring. Try serving this side dish with a roasted leg of lamb, or as part of an antipasti platter, with assorted cheeses and cured meats.

Braised Baby Artichokes

SERVES 6

- 3 lemons, 2 halved and 1 thinly sliced
- 12 baby artichokes, trimmed
- 3 cups low-sodium chicken broth, store-bought or homemade (page 256)
- 1 cup dry white wine
- 1 head garlic, peeled and cut in half crosswise
- ¼ cup extra-virgin olive oil
- 6 thyme sprigs
- 1 tablespoon coarse salt
- 1 tablespoon black peppercorns

Preheat a 5- to 6-quart slow cooker.

Fill a large bowl halfway with cold water. Squeeze lemon halves into water, then add lemons to bowl. Remove tough outer leaves from artichokes, halve artichokes, and remove any prickly chokes. Transfer halved artichokes to lemon water.

In a small saucepan, bring broth and wine to a boil over high. Place artichokes and garlic in the slow cooker. Slowly pour broth mixture over artichokes, then top with oil. Add thyme, salt, peppercorns, and lemon slices. Cover and cook on high until artichokes are tender when pierced with a knife, about 1½ hours (or on low for 3 hours). Transfer artichokes, garlic, braising liquid, and aromatics to a platter, and serve.

Tip
Don't discard the garlic. Instead, squeeze the cloves from their skins and mash them onto toasted bread, before topping with the braised artichokes.

Braised Red Cabbage

SERVES 6 TO 8

- 1 head red cabbage (about 2 pounds), cored, quartered, and sliced into ⅜-inch pieces
- 2 tablespoons extra-virgin olive oil
- 1 onion, halved and thinly sliced
- 1 teaspoon caraway seeds (optional)
- 3 to 4 tablespoons sugar, to taste
- 2 tablespoons apple cider vinegar

  Coarse salt and freshly ground pepper
- 2 firm apples, such as Granny Smith or Honeycrisp, halved, cored, and sliced

Preheat a 5- to 6-quart slow cooker.

Place cabbage in the slow cooker.

Heat oil in a large skillet over medium-low. Add onion and caraway seeds, if using, and sauté, stirring frequently, until onion is soft and just golden brown, 15 to 20 minutes.

Transfer onion to slow cooker. Add sugar, vinegar, 2 teaspoons salt, and ⅛ teaspoon pepper, and stir to combine. Fold in apples. Cover and cook on low until cabbage is tender, 5 hours (we prefer this cooked on low). Season with salt and pepper, and serve. (Cabbage can be kept warm in a slow cooker on low until ready to serve, or served at room temperature.)

Greek-Style Green Beans with Tomato

SERVES 6 TO 8

  Coarse salt and freshly ground black pepper
- 3 tablespoons extra-virgin olive oil
- 1 large onion, finely chopped
- 3 garlic cloves, thinly sliced
- ⅛ teaspoon red-pepper flakes
- 1½ teaspoons dried oregano
- 3 plum tomatoes, peeled and coarsely chopped
- 1½ pounds fresh mature green beans, trimmed and halved if large
- 1 cup low-sodium chicken broth, store-bought or homemade (page 256)
- 1 lemon, cut into wedges, for serving

Preheat a 5- to 6-quart slow cooker.

Heat oil in a large skillet over medium. Add onion and garlic, and sauté until onion is soft, about 10 minutes. Add red-pepper flakes, oregano, 1 teaspoon salt, ¼ teaspoon black pepper, and tomatoes, and sauté until tomatoes begin to break down, about 5 minutes.

Place beans and a pinch of salt in the slow cooker. Spoon tomato mixture over beans in slow cooker. Pour in broth. Cover and cook on low until beans are tender, about 3 hours. Season with salt and black pepper. Serve with lemon wedges on the side.

Corn-Chile Pudding

SERVES 6 TO 8

Unsalted butter, for slow cooker

4 cups corn kernels, fresh or frozen (thawed and drained)

1 teaspoon coarse salt

3 scallions (white and pale green parts only), thinly sliced, plus more for serving

1 can (4 ounces) diced green chiles, or 4 to 5 large poblano chiles, roasted

¾ cup diced Black Forest ham

3 tablespoons all-purpose flour

6 ounces (2 cups) grated manchego cheese or extra-sharp white cheddar

5 large eggs, room temperature

⅔ cup heavy cream

Butter the insert of a 5- to 6-quart slow cooker.

Puree 3 cups corn in a blender or food processor. Transfer to a large bowl and stir in remaining 1 cup corn, the salt, scallions, chiles, ham, flour, and 1 cup cheese.

In another bowl, whisk together eggs and cream just until combined. Stir into corn mixture. Pour batter into the slow cooker and top with remaining 1 cup cheese. Cover and cook on low until pudding is set, 2 hours (do not cook on high), uncovering for last 15 minutes. Let cool 30 minutes before serving, topped with sliced scallions.

Smoky Collard Greens with Tofu

SERVES 6 TO 8

¼ cup canola or safflower oil

¾ cup finely chopped sweet onion (1 large onion)

4 ounces smoked or regular firm tofu, cut into 1-inch pieces

2 bunches collard greens (about 1 pound each), tough stems and ribs removed, leaves cut into ½-inch ribbons

¾ cup barbecue sauce, store-bought or homemade (page 266)

¼ cup apple cider vinegar

Coarse salt and freshly ground pepper

3 cups boiling water

Preheat a 5- to 6-quart slow cooker.

Heat 2 tablespoons oil in a large skillet over high. Add onion and tofu, and cook until lightly browned, about 8 minutes. Transfer to the slow cooker.

In same skillet, heat 1 tablespoon oil over high. In two batches, cook collards until wilted, adding remaining tablespoon oil between batches.

Transfer collards to the slow cooker. Stir in barbecue sauce and vinegar, and season with salt and pepper. Add the boiling water, cover, and cook on high until very tender, 4 hours (or on low for 8 hours). Season with salt and pepper, and serve.

For this Mediterranean-style side dish, we initially tried slow-cooking raw fennel in broth and oil. But we were not satisfied with the resulting flavor until we first browned the fennel on the stovetop, then slow-cooked it with the the liquids and aromatics.

Braised Fennel with Olives and Peppers

SERVES 4 TO 6

3 to 4 tablespoons extra-virgin olive oil

5 fennel bulbs, cored and cut into wedges, with fronds reserved

Coarse salt and freshly ground pepper

2 large garlic cloves, thinly sliced

1 teaspoon dried oregano

Juice of 1 lemon

1 cup low-sodium chicken broth, store-bought or homemade (page 256)

2 tablespoons capers, rinsed and drained

⅓ cup pitted green olives, such as Sicilian or Castelvetrano, sliced in half

2 teaspoons chopped fresh thyme

1½ teaspoons chopped fresh rosemary

1 large red bell pepper, roasted (see instructions, page 267)

Preheat a 5- to 6-quart slow cooker.

Heat 1½ tablespoons oil in a large skillet over medium-high. Working in batches, add half the fennel, cut sides down, and sauté until golden brown, 2 to 3 minutes. Turn fennel, with tongs, and brown on other sides, 2 to 3 more minutes. Transfer fennel to the slow cooker. Season with salt and pepper. Repeat with 1½ tablespoons oil and remaining fennel.

In a skillet, add up to 1 tablespoon more oil, if necessary, and reduce heat to medium-low. Add garlic and oregano to skillet, and cook 1 minute. Add lemon juice, ½ cup broth, capers, and olives; simmer 2 minutes.

Pour olive mixture over fennel. Sprinkle with thyme and rosemary. Add remaining ½ cup broth. Cover and cook on high until fennel is very tender but not falling apart, 4 hours (or on low for 8 hours).

About 30 minutes before fennel is ready, remove lid, add roasted pepper, and cook, uncovered, until pepper is heated through. Serve warm.

When we tested slow-cooked broccoli with cheese sauce side by side with cauliflower prepared the same way, we much preferred the latter. It holds up well as it slow-cooks in this rich béchamel, made with two cheeses (and just a hint of anchovy, which is essential to getting the right flavor).

Cauliflower with Cream Sauce

SERVES 4

4 tablespoons unsalted butter

1 small onion, minced

2 garlic cloves, minced

⅓ cup all-purpose flour

1 cup milk

1 cup heavy cream

½ cup finely grated Parmigiano-Reggiano cheese (2 ounces)

¼ cup finely grated Pecorino Romano cheese (1 ounce), plus more for serving

Coarse salt and freshly ground black pepper

¼ teaspoon freshly grated nutmeg

¼ teaspoon red-pepper flakes

½ teaspoon finely grated lemon zest

2 small anchovy fillets, minced

2 pounds cauliflower, cut into florets

1¼ cups coarse fresh breadcrumbs (see page 267)

1 tablespoon olive oil

¼ cup plus 2 tablespoons minced fresh flat-leaf parsley

Preheat a 5- to 6-quart slow cooker.

Melt butter in a skillet over medium heat. Add onion and cook, stirring occasionally, until almost soft, about 4 minutes. Add garlic and cook 2 minutes longer, until onion and garlic are soft. Stir in flour and cook 1 minute. Whisk in milk and cream. Bring to a simmer and cook, stirring, until slightly thickened, about 2 minutes. Stir in both cheeses, ½ teaspoon salt, ½ teaspoon black pepper, nutmeg, red-pepper flakes, and lemon zest; cook 1 minute. Remove from heat and stir in anchovies. Season with salt and black pepper. Place cauliflower in the slow cooker and season with salt and black pepper. Pour sauce over cauliflower and toss to coat. Cook on low until cauliflower is fork-tender, 2 hours (or on high for 1 hour), stirring once or twice.

Preheat oven to 450°F. Toss breadcrumbs with oil, and season with salt and black pepper. Spread mixture in a single layer on a small rimmed baking sheet and toast, stirring halfway through, until breadcrumbs are golden, about 8 minutes. Transfer to a wire rack and let cool; mix in minced parsley.

Transfer cauliflower to a platter, garnish with breadcrumbs, Pecorino, and parsley, and serve.

In this familiar dish, a few humble ingredients are transformed into something truly luxurious. Keep scalloped potatoes in mind for any holiday meal, alongside any kind of roast—turkey, beef, lamb, you name it. Resist the urge to lift the lid as the potatoes cook; it may look as if they are separating from the cream sauce, but both will come together in the end.

Scalloped Potatoes

SERVES 6 TO 8

- 3 tablespoons unsalted butter, plus more for slow cooker
- 1 sweet onion, finely chopped

  Coarse salt and freshly ground black pepper
- 1 tablespoon minced garlic
- ¼ cup all-purpose flour
- 1½ cups half-and-half
- 1 teaspoon dry mustard

  Pinch cayenne pepper
- 1 teaspoon fresh thyme leaves, plus 2 sprigs
- 2 cups coarsely grated Gruyère cheese (8 ounces)
- 8 Yukon Gold potatoes (about 2½ pounds), peeled and sliced paper-thin

Butter the insert of a 5- to 6-quart slow cooker.

In a large saucepan, melt butter over medium heat. Add onion and sauté until translucent, about 8 minutes. Season with salt. Add garlic and cook 1 minute more. Add flour and cook, stirring constantly, about 2 minutes. Gradually whisk in half-and-half; cook, stirring, until sauce thickens and comes to a boil. Add mustard, ½ teaspoon salt, ¼ teaspoon black pepper, cayenne, 1 teaspoon thyme, and 1 cup cheese. Reduce heat and continue whisking 2 to 3 minutes more. Remove from heat.

Season potatoes with salt and black pepper. Layer half the potatoes evenly on bottom of the slow cooker, overlapping slightly. Pour half the cheese sauce over layer, spreading to cover evenly. Repeat layering potatoes and cheese sauce. Sprinkle with remaining 1 cup cheese and the thyme sprigs. Cover and cook on low until potatoes are tender when pierced with a knife, 6 to 7 hours (or on high for 3 to 3½ hours). Remove lid and allow potatoes to rest for 15 minutes before serving.

Here's an example of how well sweet (squash, dates, maple syrup) and savory (shallots, thyme, red-pepper flakes) flavors can complement one another in one delicious dish. This is a natural partner for roast chicken, turkey, or pork, but it also makes a wonderful vegetarian main course, with simply dressed kale and a few goat cheese–topped crostini.

Winter Squash with Shallots and Dates

SERVES 4 TO 6

2 small acorn squash (about 2 pounds), halved, seeded, and cut into wedges

6 shallots, quartered

10 Medjool dates, pitted and thinly sliced

6 thyme sprigs

¼ cup plus 2 tablespoons extra-virgin olive oil

¼ cup pure maple syrup

1 teaspoon coarse salt

⅛ teaspoon freshly ground black pepper

⅛ teaspoon red-pepper flakes

Preheat a 5- to 6-quart slow cooker.

Combine squash, shallots, dates, and thyme in a large bowl. Drizzle with oil and maple syrup, and sprinkle with salt, black pepper, and red-pepper flakes. Toss well with your hands, then transfer to the slow cooker. Cover and cook on high, turning squash once or twice during cooking, until squash is tender, about 3 hours (or on low for 6 hours). Transfer to a large bowl and serve.

Tip
You don't need to peel acorn squash before cooking or eating, making this preparation especially quick. You can substitute wedges of other types of winter squash, including butternut; but you'll need to peel those before putting them in the slow cooker.

Next time you are baking a ham for Sunday supper, or roasting a pork shoulder, or even just planning to throw some hot dogs on the grill, keep this sensational side dish in mind. The beans develop their characteristic rich, deep flavor over several hours in the slow cooker.

Cider Baked Beans

SERVES 6 TO 8

3 cups dried great northern beans, picked over and rinsed

6 slices bacon, cut into 1-inch pieces

1 large onion, finely chopped

⅓ cup tomato paste

2 tablespoons Worcestershire sauce

3 tablespoons Dijon mustard

½ cup packed dark brown sugar

2 tablespoons apple cider vinegar

½ teaspoon cayenne pepper

2 dried bay leaves

3 to 4 cups fresh apple cider, as needed

Coarse salt and freshly ground black pepper

Place beans in a large bowl; cover with water by several inches. Refrigerate, covered, overnight; drain. (To quick soak, cover beans in a large saucepan with water. Bring to a boil. Remove from heat. Let stand, covered, for 1 hour; drain.)

Preheat a 5- to 6-quart slow cooker.

In a large skillet over medium-high heat, cook bacon until crisp, 5 to 7 minutes. Using a slotted spoon, transfer bacon to a paper-towel-lined plate. Pour off all but 2 tablespoons fat from skillet, reduce heat to medium-low, and add onion. Cook until translucent, about 15 minutes. Stir in tomato paste; then raise heat to medium and simmer for 5 minutes. Add Worcestershire, mustard, brown sugar, vinegar, cayenne, bay leaves, and 3 cups apple cider. Stir well to combine and simmer until thickened slightly, for 10 minutes. Remove from heat; add 1 teaspoon salt and ¼ teaspoon black pepper.

Add beans to the slow cooker and toss with cider sauce. Pour cider sauce over beans and stir to combine. If necessary, add up to 1 cup more cider to cover beans. Cover and cook on low until beans are tender, 6 to 7 hours (or on high for 3 to 3½ hours). Season with salt and black pepper, and serve.

Breakfast

Maple Granola, page 215

The Basics

It's easy to motivate yourself to wake up and cook a big breakfast when you have extra hands to help you. But when you're planning a brunch, or you have guests, the slow cooker is all the help you need. To get a head start, simply mix a few ingredients and turn on the heat for a few hours. Later, you'll come back to discover ultra-rich French toast flecked with apple and brown sugar, or creamy grits to top with braised greens, or perfectly cooked congee, the traditional Chinese rice porridge that you can finish with any number of savory additions (we love it with tender white fish). Or, if you'd really just love to sleep a bit late, prepare oatmeal that cooks overnight, then serve it with a spectrum of accompaniments—say, apricots roasted with a splash of Grand Marnier. Offer a few options, and let guests customize their own bowls.

Of course, the slow cooker makes a mean porridge. But you'll be more surprised at the ingenious ways it can be used for all kinds of breakfast possibilities—like a Croque Monsieur Strata with Gruyère cheese, ham, and grainy mustard, or the wonderfully hearty and homey Hash Brown Casserole.

One thing that you will not find here are many slow-cooked egg dishes. As much as we love quiches and frittatas for breakfast and brunch, we simply couldn't get behind the texture of them when cooked in the machine. Instead, we opted to fry or poach a few eggs on the stove, then use them to top individual servings of grits and greens, for example. The exception are the eggs that poach right in our slow-cooked tomato sauce; the texture turned out just fine, as the cooking time was kept to a minimum.

Finally, as much as the slow cooker is meant for moist-heat cooking, you can also use it to "bake." Try the toasty, wholesome granola—the secret is leaving the lid partially off. Or try the most mind-bendingly easy and delicious cinnamon buns. No matter what you decide to make, it's entirely possible you'll have the meal well under way even before you've poured your first cup of coffee.

Recipes

Grits with Greens and Fried Eggs

Maple Granola

Eggs Poached in Tomato Sauce

Cinnamon Buns

Overnight Oatmeal

Croque Monsieur Strata

Congee with Fish

Hash Brown Casserole

Apple French Toast

When you have a house full of guests, keep grits in mind, as they're so hearty and substantial that a little goes a long way toward feeding a crowd. Try serving the grits assembly-line style, straight from the slow cooker, with braised collards, fried eggs, and hot sauce on the side.

Grits with Greens and Fried Eggs

SERVES 8

2 cups white hominy grits (not quick-cooking)

4½ cups hot water

4 cups milk

Coarse salt

4 ounces cotija or feta cheese, crumbled (1 cup)

2 tablespoons extra-virgin olive oil

1 small onion, thinly sliced

6 garlic cloves, thinly sliced

¼ teaspoon red-pepper flakes

1 bunch collard greens (about 1 pound), tough stems and ribs removed, leaves coarsely chopped

Fried eggs, for serving

Hot sauce, for serving

Preheat a 5- to 6-quart slow cooker.

Stir to combine grits with 4 cups hot water, the milk, and 2 teaspoons salt in the slow cooker. Cover and cook, stirring occasionally, on high until grits are creamy, 3 hours (or on low for 6 hours). Stir in cheese and season with salt.

Meanwhile heat oil in a large skillet over medium. Add onion and cook until translucent, about 3 minutes. Add garlic and cook, stirring often, until golden, about 3 minutes. Stir in red-pepper flakes and cook until fragrant, about 30 seconds.

Stir in collard greens and 1 teaspoon salt. Reduce heat to medium-low. Add remaining ½ cup hot water, cover, and steam until greens are just tender and water evaporates, about 10 minutes. (If greens are ready but there is still water in the pan, raise heat to medium-high, and cook, uncovered, until completely evaporated.)

Serve grits with greens, eggs, and hot sauce.

For a crisp and crunchy mix, slow-cook granola on the machine's high setting, as it tends to dry out on low; it's also crucial to cover it only partially, and rotate the lid to allow moisture to escape as it cooks. This recipe is not too sweet and gets a nice, rich flavor from olive oil.

Maple Granola

MAKES 5 TO 6 CUPS

¾ cup extra-virgin olive oil, plus more for slow cooker

4 cups old-fashioned rolled oats

1 cup raw shelled pistachios, almonds, walnuts, pecans, or hazelnuts, chopped if large

¼ cup packed brown sugar

½ teaspoon ground cinnamon

½ teaspoon coarse salt

½ cup pure maple syrup

1 tablespoon vanilla extract

½ cup dried apricots, dates, cherries, figs, raisins, blueberries, or cranberries, chopped if large

Brush the insert of a 5- to 6-quart slow cooker with oil and preheat cooker.

Stir together oats, nuts, brown sugar, cinnamon, and ¼ teaspoon salt in the slow cooker until well combined. Stir in oil, maple syrup, and vanilla, mixing until fully combined. Raise heat to high, partially cover, turning lid 45 degrees to allow moisture to escape, and cook on high, stirring every 30 minutes, until toasted and golden brown, about 2 hours (do not cook on low). After 1 hour, rotate cooker insert 180 degrees to prevent scorching.

Stir in dried fruit; then spread granola in a single layer on a rimmed baking sheet to cool completely. Sprinkle with remaining ¼ teaspoon salt, if desired. (Store in an airtight container at room temperature for up to 1 week.)

The Italians call this dish "eggs in purgatory." It bears a strong resemblance to shakshuka, the Israeli breakfast of eggs cooked in spicy tomato sauce. Using the slow cooker means you can start the sauce the night before and cook the eggs the next morning, as well as toast some bread and brew a pot of coffee to serve alongside.

Eggs Poached in Tomato Sauce

SERVES 4

2 pounds ripe plum tomatoes, cored, blanched, peeled, and seeded

4 garlic cloves, smashed and peeled

¼ cup extra-virgin olive oil

4 basil sprigs

Coarse salt and freshly ground pepper

Pinch sugar

½ cup boiling water

4 large eggs

Fresh herbs, such as oregano or basil, for garnish

Preheat a 5- to 6-quart slow cooker.

Add tomatoes, garlic, oil, basil, 1 teaspoon salt, ¼ teaspoon pepper, and sugar to the slow cooker, stirring to combine. Add the boiling water. Cover and cook on high for 1 hour. Reduce heat to low and cook 4 hours more. (For a thicker sauce, continue cooking on low 2 additional hours, or until desired thickness is reached.)

Use a spoon to create 4 shallow wells in tomato sauce. Gently crack 1 egg into each well, and cook until set, 8 to 10 minutes. Season with salt and pepper. Serve topped with herbs.

The scent of fresh cinnamon buns is a joy to wake up to. These are made with a very easy quick-rise yeasted dough rolled around a sugary, sweet-spicy filling, and finished with a drizzly glaze.

Cinnamon Buns

SERVES 10 TO 12

FOR BUNS

6 tablespoons unsalted butter, room temperature, plus more for brushing

1⅓ cups warm water (about 110°F)

1 tablespoon active dry yeast

2 tablespoons honey

3½ cups all-purpose flour, plus more for work surface

1 teaspoon coarse salt

¾ cup granulated sugar

¼ cup plus 2 tablespoons packed brown sugar

1 tablespoon ground cinnamon

FOR GLAZE

3 cups confectioners' sugar

Juice of ½ lemon

1 teaspoon vanilla extract

¼ cup plus 2 tablespoons milk

Make buns: Brush the insert of a 5- to 6-quart slow cooker with butter. Line bottom with parchment paper and brush paper with butter.

Combine the warm water, yeast, and honey in a bowl; let stand until foamy, about 5 minutes. Add flour and salt. With an electric mixer on low, mix until just combined. Increase speed to medium and mix for 5 minutes; let stand 10 minutes. Combine butter, both sugars, and cinnamon in a bowl; mix until smooth.

Preheat the slow cooker. Turn dough out onto a lightly floured work surface and roll into a rectangle, about 9 by 15 inches. Sprinkle dough evenly with cinnamon-sugar mixture. Starting from one long side, roll into a log, pinching seams to seal in filling. Slice log into 10 to 12 rounds, each about 1½ inches thick.

Arrange rolls, cut side down, in the cooker. Wrap lid tightly with a clean kitchen towel, gathering ends at top (to absorb condensation). Cover and cook on high until cooked through, 1½ hours (we prefer to bake these on high). After 1 hour, rotate cooker insert 180 degrees to prevent scorching. Turn out onto a wire rack to cool before serving.

Make glaze: With an electric mixer, whisk confectioners' sugar, lemon juice, and vanilla until smooth. Slowly add ¼ cup milk and beat on medium. Add more milk, a drop at a time up to 2 tablespoons, to reach desired consistency. Drizzle rolls with glaze just before serving.

This may just become your new favorite breakfast, since the oats cook to the ideal texture while you sleep. They also take well to any number of toppings, savory or sweet. Swirl Greek yogurt into the oats, top with roasted apricots and golden raisins; then drizzle with maple syrup. For savory oatmeal, omit the vanilla bean and sugar.

Overnight Oatmeal

SERVES 4

1 cup steel-cut oats

4½ cups boiling water

¼ cup packed light brown or raw sugar

1 vanilla bean, split lengthwise, seeds scraped

⅛ teaspoon coarse salt

Roasted Apricots

Maple syrup, yogurt, and golden raisins (optional), for serving

Tip
Instead of cooking the oats in water, you can use a mixture of half milk and half water, or a cow's-milk alternative such as almond or coconut milk.

Preheat a 5- to 6-quart slow cooker.

Combine oats, the boiling water, sugar, vanilla bean and seeds, and salt in the slow cooker. Cover and cook on low 8 hours (or on high for 4 hours). Remove and discard vanilla bean before serving.

Roasted Apricots: Preheat oven to 350°F. In a roasting dish, place 8 halved, pitted **apricots** with 4 tablespoons **unsalted butter**, ¼ cup **raw sugar**, and 1 teaspoon **Grand Marnier**. Roast until apricots are tender, about 30 minutes.

Rye bread, ham, Gruyère, and grainy mustard are layered and soaked in a simple egg custard before slow-cooking to savory perfection. Prep the ingredients the night before, then plug in the machine when you awake. Four hours later, you'll have the ultimate Sunday brunch dish ready and waiting. Top each serving with a fried egg to make it a croque madame.

Croque Monsieur Strata

SERVES 8

- 2 tablespoons olive oil, plus more for brushing
- 1 pound thick-cut ham, cut into ⅓-inch cubes
- 3 cups coarsely grated Gruyère or Swiss cheese (12 ounces)
  Coarse salt and freshly ground pepper
- 10 slices sourdough bread
- 2 garlic cloves
- 3 tablespoons whole-grain mustard
- ¼ cup snipped chives
- 10 large eggs
- 2¾ cups milk

Brush the insert of a 5- to 6-quart slow cooker with oil. Add a foil strip to the back wall to prevent scorching and make a foil sling (see page 15); brush or spray foil with oil. Preheat the slow cooker.

In a large bowl, combine ham and 2 cups cheese; season generously with pepper.

Preheat oven to 450°F. Brush one side of bread lightly with oil. Toast directly on oven rack until lightly golden, 8 to 10 minutes. Rub both sides with garlic, spread mustard on one side, and top with chives. Arrange 2 to 3 bread slices, mustard sides up, in the slow cooker, breaking up slices to fill gaps. Cover with half the ham-and-cheese mixture. Repeat layering, ending with bread, mustard side up.

In bowl, whisk eggs, milk, and 1½ teaspoons salt. Pour egg mixture over bread and let soak 30 minutes, pressing down on bread to help absorb liquid. Cover slow cooker and cook on low for 4 hours.

Preheat oven to 450°F. Using the sling as handles, lift bread pudding from insert and transfer to a rimmed baking sheet. Sprinkle remaining 1 cup cheese over top of bread, transfer to oven, and bake bread pudding until golden, about 15 minutes. Let rest 15 minutes. Remove foil and cut bread pudding into wedges.

The Chinese slow-cooked rice dish known as congee, or jook, may not spring to mind as a breakfast option. But if you've never tried it, the slow cooker provides the perfect opportunity to do so. Like oatmeal, it's easy to prepare, and you can finish it any way you like. We're partial to fish congee, topped with peanuts, scallions, soy sauce, toasted sesame oil, sesame seeds, and Sriracha; rice vinegar, bonito flakes, and chopped cilantro are nice, too.

Congee with Fish

SERVES 6

1½ cups long-grain white rice

1 (1-inch) piece fresh ginger, peeled and grated

3 quarts boiling water

12 ounces firm white fish fillets, such as flounder or cod, skin removed, thinly sliced

Coarse salt

Suggested toppings:
Roasted peanuts, sliced scallions, toasted sesame oil, sesame seeds, hot sauce, rice vinegar, bonito flakes, chopped fresh cilantro, and soy sauce, for serving

Preheat a 5- to 6-quart slow cooker on low. Transfer rice and ginger to the slow cooker. Add the boiling water and stir. Cover and cook on low until congee reaches consistency of loose porridge, about 4 hours (or on high for 2 hours).

Add fish and cook on low until fish falls apart, about 20 minutes more (or on high for 10 minutes). Season with salt. Serve immediately in bowls, with suggested toppings.

With sausages, cheddar cheese, potatoes, and fried eggs, this makes an incredibly hearty, one-stop breakfast. In fact, it's so rich and indulgent, you may want to reserve it for very special occasions.

Hash Brown Casserole

SERVES 6 TO 8

2   tablespoons unsalted butter

2   tablespoons all-purpose flour

¾   cup low-sodium chicken broth, store-bought or homemade (page 256)

½   cup milk

   Coarse salt and freshly ground pepper

1   pound sweet Italian sausage, casings removed

3   sweet peppers, such as Cubanelle, thinly sliced

2   pounds russet potatoes, peeled and grated on large holes of a box grater

1   cup grated cheddar cheese (4 ounces)

6   scallions, finely chopped

   Fried eggs, for serving

   Snipped fresh chives, for garnish

Melt butter in a saucepan over medium heat. Whisk in flour and cook about 1 minute. Add broth and milk, and bring to a boil, whisking constantly. Remove from heat, and season with salt and pepper. Transfer sauce to a bowl.

Heat saucepan over medium-high. Add sausage and cook, breaking up meat with a spoon, until browned, about 5 minutes. Add peppers and continue to cook on high until peppers are soft, about 5 minutes. Season with salt and pepper. Transfer to a 5- to 6-quart slow cooker, spreading into an even layer.

Add potatoes, cheese, and scallions to milk mixture and mix well. Transfer to slow cooker and spread into an even layer. Cover and cook on high until hot and bubbly, about 3 hours (or on low for 6 hours). Serve warm, with fried eggs and topped with chives.

The ultimate sleepover breakfast, this casserole is no worse for wear after soaking overnight. In the morning, it cooks in a couple of hours and can be kept warm on a low setting for any breakfast stragglers. Offer a side of crisp bacon for a salty, smoky contrast to the sweet French toast.

Apple French Toast

SERVES 6 TO 8

¾ cup (1½ sticks) unsalted butter, room temperature, plus more for brushing

1½ cups packed brown sugar

2 teaspoons ground cinnamon

8 large eggs

1½ cups milk

¾ cup heavy cream, plus more for drizzling

1 teaspoon vanilla extract

2 tablespoons pure maple syrup

Pinch coarse salt

1 large apple, such as Granny Smith or Cortland, peeled and cut into ½-inch dice

1 pound challah, cut into 2-inch pieces

Brush the insert of a 5- to 6-quart slow cooker with butter.

Using a fork, combine butter, brown sugar, and cinnamon in a small bowl until fine crumbs form. In another bowl, whisk together eggs, milk, cream, vanilla, maple syrup, and salt.

Sprinkle one-third of butter-sugar mixture in slow-cooker insert. Top with diced apple. Cover apple with half the bread pieces, then one-third of butter mixture. Top with remaining bread and sprinkle with remaining butter mixture. Pour egg mixture over bread and gently press down to fully submerge bread. Let chill, covered, at least 2 hours and up to overnight.

Place insert in slow cooker, cover, and cook on high until center of mixture is set, about 2 hours and 15 minutes (or on low for about 4½ hours). Serve warm, with cream on the side for drizzling.

Sweets

Crème Brûlée,
page 238

The Basics

Dessert from the slow cooker is a waiting game—anywhere from two to eight hours. But it is well worth it, not only for how much of the time is hands-off but also for how delectable the results are. It's a revelation, for instance, how moist and delicious Sticky Toffee Pudding can be when steamed in the machine. For a dinner party, serving a low-and-slow four-hour Apple-Cranberry Crisp allows you the luxury of lingering at the table. All you have to do after dinner is scoop the warm fruit dessert into deep bowls and top with vanilla ice cream.

You'll find the slow cooker a handy problem-solver, too: On holidays, it's indispensable for handling the dessert course when the oven is fully occupied. And during the dog days of summer, you can bake a fresh Blueberry Cornmeal Buckle in the slow cooker without having to turn on the oven.

The crock is just what you need to make the most luscious custards and the gold standard of cheesecakes—meaning one with a crack-free top. For these desserts, the trick is to place the pan inside the cooker's insert, atop a few balls of aluminum foil set in boiling water; then to wrap the lid with a clean kitchen towel. The result is a creamy, super-smooth finish. Next up: making one again, immediately.

In fact, the more you make desserts with the slow cooker, the more you'll be tempted to play around with variations. Once you see how beautifully pears poach in the machine, for example, you'll be tempted to try the same technique with rhubarb in the springtime or peaches at the peak of summer. Then, you can round out the course with the accompaniment of your choice: pound cake, crème fraîche, a few shortbread cookies, or maybe even nothing at all.

Recipes

Cheesecake

Rice Pudding

Crème Brûlée

Apple-Cranberry Crisp

Blueberry Cornmeal Buckle

Sticky Toffee Pudding

Peach-Pecan Grunt

Butterscotch Bread Pudding with Brown-Butter Rum Sauce

Wine-Poached Pears

Slow-cooker cheesecake is a dream: The heat is gentle and steady, and the resting period allows a gradual cool-down, eliminating the cracked top of most home-baked cheesecakes.

Cheesecake

SERVES 6

Nonstick cooking spray

FOR CRUST

- ¾ cup graham cracker crumbs
- 2 tablespoons unsalted butter, melted
- 2 tablespoons sugar

FOR FILLING

- 16 ounces cream cheese, softened
- ½ cup sugar
- 2 tablespoons all-purpose flour
- 1 teaspoon vanilla extract
- 2 large eggs, room temperature
- ½ cup plain yogurt or sour cream

VARIATIONS

Marbled: Use **chocolate wafers** in place of grahams. Melt 2 ounces **bittersweet chocolate**; mix into ½ cup batter and dollop onto filling in pan. Run a knife tip through dollops to marbleize top. Or melt 3 tablespoons **seedless raspberry jam**; drop ½-inch dots onto filling; swirl with a toothpick. Bake as directed.

Pumpkin: Use **gingersnaps** in place of grahams. Increase sugar in batter to ½ cup plus 2 tablespoons and flour to 3 tablespoons. Add 2 teaspoons **pumpkin pie spice** and ⅔ cup canned **pumpkin puree**. Omit yogurt. Bake as directed.

Lightly coat a 6-inch springform pan with cooking spray; line bottom with parchment and lightly spray. Fill a 5- to 6-quart slow cooker with ½ inch hot water. Set three 1-inch balls of foil in center of slow cooker. Wrap slow-cooker lid tightly with a clean kitchen towel, gathering ends at top (to absorb condensation).

Make crust: Combine crumbs, butter, and sugar. Press mixture evenly on bottom and about 1 inch up sides of springform pan.

Make filling: In a food processor, pulse cream cheese, sugar, flour, and vanilla until smooth. Add eggs and process until combined. Add yogurt and process until smooth, scraping down sides of bowl. Pour filling into pan. Gently tap pan on work surface to remove air bubbles.

Set pan on aluminum balls in slow cooker. Cover and cook on high until set and an instant-read thermometer inserted in center registers 155°F, 1½ to 2 hours (do not cook on low). Turn off slow cooker and let cake rest, covered, 1 hour.

Carefully transfer pan to a wire rack to cool completely, then refrigerate until chilled, at least 4 hours and preferably overnight. Carefully remove outer ring from pan and transfer cake to a plate (remove parchment). Use a warm knife to cut into wedges, wiping blade after each cut.

Chocolate Marbled
Cheesecake

Rice doesn't benefit from the heat of the slow cooker—it doesn't hold its texture properly and the grains don't stay intact. For the same reasons, the slow cooker is excellent for making rice pudding (or its cousin, congee; see page 224). Medium- or short-grain rice works best for this dessert.

Rice Pudding

SERVES 6 TO 8

Unsalted butter, melted, for slow cooker

6 cups milk

1 vanilla bean, split lengthwise, seeds scraped

⅔ cup sugar

1 teaspoon ground cinnamon, plus more for garnish

Pinch coarse salt

2 cardamom pods, crushed

1 cup medium-grain rice, such as Arborio

Fresh fruit, such as raspberries, for serving (optional)

Brush the insert of a 5- to 6-quart slow cooker with melted butter and preheat the slow cooker.

Combine milk, vanilla bean and seeds, sugar, cinnamon, salt, and cardamom pods in a saucepan, and bring mixture to a simmer over medium heat; stir in rice. Remove vanilla bean and cardamom pods. Transfer mixture to the slow cooker. Cover and cook until rice is tender, 1¾ to 2 hours on high (or on low for 3 to 4 hours), stirring after 1 hour.

Serve rice pudding in bowls, topped with fruit (if using) and cinnamon.

Tip

Infusing cinnamon and cardamom in rice pudding from the outset adds hints of warm and wonderful flavor. Try experimenting with other flavoring agents, including finely grated orange or lemon zest, almond extract, or rum-soaked golden raisins. Afterward, garnish servings with fresh fruit, chopped almonds or other nuts, toasted coconut flakes, or honey.

The appeal of crème brûlée (French for "burnt cream") lies in the contrast between the brittle caramelized topping and the smooth, rich custard beneath. This dessert is best served immediately after caramelizing its sweet, sugary surface with the quick swipe of a kitchen blowtorch.

Crème Brûlée

SERVES 8

Boiling water, for slow cooker

4 cups heavy cream

¾ cup granulated sugar

1 vanilla bean, split lengthwise and seeds scraped

7 large egg yolks

¼ teaspoon coarse salt

½ cup superfine sugar, for topping

Set a 1½-quart soufflé dish into a 5- to 6-quart slow cooker. Pour enough boiling water into slow cooker to reach halfway up the sides of soufflé dish.

Combine cream, 6 tablespoons granulated sugar, and vanilla bean and seeds into a saucepan and heat over medium just until bubbles start to form around edges, 7 to 8 minutes (do not boil).

Whisk yolks with remaining 6 tablespoons granulated sugar and the salt, in a large bowl. Gently whisk a small amount of cream mixture into egg mixture to combine. Add 2 more ladles of cream mixture, one at a time, whisking to combine after each. Gradually whisk in remaining cream mixture. Strain custard through a fine sieve into a large measuring cup (discard solids). Pour custard into dish.

Cover slow cooker and cook on high until custard is just set, about 2½ hours (or on low for 5 hours). Turn off slow cooker, remove lid, and let custard stand until water is cool enough to remove dish. Let cool completely, cover with plastic wrap, and refrigerate, at least 2 hours and up to 3 days.

Sprinkle superfine sugar over custard. Pass the flame of a kitchen torch in a circular motion 1 to 2 inches above custard until sugar bubbles and turns amber. Serve immediately.

The secret to getting a crisp to *actually* crisp in the slow cooker is to wrap the machine's lid in a towel to absorb condensation, and to leave the lid slightly ajar throughout the cooking time. Ice cream is the classic accompaniment to rustic fruit desserts like this one, but crème fraîche or whole-milk yogurt are other nice options.

Apple-Cranberry Crisp

SERVES 6 TO 8

FOR FILLING

- 3 pounds Granny Smith apples, peeled, cored, and cut into ¾-inch pieces
- 1 cup fresh or frozen cranberries
- ¾ cup granulated sugar
- 1 tablespoon cornstarch
- 2 tablespoons unsalted butter, cut into small cubes

FOR TOPPING

- 1 cup all-purpose flour
- 1 teaspoon ground cinnamon
- 1 teaspoon coarse salt
- ¼ cup packed light brown sugar
- 2 tablespoons granulated sugar
- 6 tablespoons cold unsalted butter, cut into small cubes
- 1 cup old-fashioned rolled oats (not quick-cooking)
- ¼ cup finely chopped pecans

   Ice cream, for serving

Make filling: Combine apples, cranberries, sugar, cornstarch, and butter in a 5- to 6-quart slow cooker; let sit 10 minutes. Stir to mix, and then press into an even layer in slow cooker.

Make topping: Combine flour, cinnamon, salt, and both sugars. Cut in butter with a pastry blender, working mixture until it resembles coarse meal. Add oats and pecans, and press into small clumps.

Scatter topping over filling in cooker. Wrap slow-cooker lid tightly with a clean kitchen towel, gathering the ends at top (to absorb condensation). Cover, leaving lid slightly ajar so steam can escape, and cook on high until bubbling and crisp, 4 hours (or on low for 8 hours); rotate slow cooker insert 180 degrees halfway through cooking to prevent scorching. Let crisp sit uncovered at least 10 minutes before serving with ice cream.

Tip
Vanilla ice cream is delicious here, as is salted caramel, cinnamon, or buttermilk.

A buttery brown-sugar streusel tops this easy crumb cake before it bakes. If you really want to take it over the top, drizzle the cooled cake with glaze: Simply whisk together two-thirds cup confectioners' sugar, three tablespoons heavy cream or milk, and half a teaspoon vanilla until smooth.

Blueberry Cornmeal Buckle

SERVES 6 TO 8

Nonstick baking spray

FOR BATTER

1¼ cups all-purpose flour

¾ cup fine yellow cornmeal

1½ teaspoons baking powder

¼ teaspoon baking soda

1 teaspoon coarse salt

½ cup (1 stick) unsalted butter, room temperature

1 cup granulated sugar

1 teaspoon vanilla extract

2 large eggs

¾ cup buttermilk, preferably full-fat

1 cup blueberries

FOR STREUSEL

½ cup all-purpose flour

3 tablespoons light brown sugar

3 tablespoons unsalted butter, room temperature

½ teaspoon ground cinnamon

Lightly coat the insert of a 4-quart slow cooker with baking spray. Line bottom with parchment and spray.

Make batter: Whisk together flour, cornmeal, baking powder, baking soda, and salt in a bowl. With an electric mixer on medium, beat butter, sugar, and vanilla until pale and fluffy, 3 to 5 minutes. Beat in eggs, one at a time. Add flour mixture in three batches, alternating with buttermilk; beat until combined.

Transfer batter to slow cooker; smooth top with an offset spatula. Top with blueberries. Wrap lid with a clean kitchen towel, gathering the ends at top (to absorb condensation). Cover and cook on high for 2 hours (or on low for 4 hours); cake will be undercooked. Rotate 180 degrees halfway through for even baking.

Make streusel: In a small bowl, combine flour, brown sugar, butter, and cinnamon. Using a fork, mix butter into flour mixture until fine crumbs form. Using your hands, squeeze together the mixture to form large clumps.

Scatter streusel on top of cake, concentrating mixture around edges. Cover and cook on high until a tester inserted in center comes out clean, 1 to 1½ hours longer (or on low for 2 to 3 hours). Cool in pan for 15 minutes, then invert onto a cutting board; invert again onto a wire rack to cool completely, right side up.

Sweet dreams are truly made of this—our kitchen team's favorite slow-cooker dessert. Using a water bath (or bain-marie) produces the dreamiest texture—not too dense and not too light. Don't skimp on the toffee-sauce-and-pecan finish. If your slow cooker cannot accommodate a soufflé dish, try baking this in ramekins.

Sticky Toffee Pudding

SERVES 6 TO 8

FOR PUDDING

- 4 tablespoons unsalted butter, melted, plus more for dish
- 2 rounded teaspoons instant espresso
- 1 cup boiling water, plus more for slow cooker
- 8 ounces Medjool dates, pitted and finely chopped (about 1½ cups)
- 1 teaspoon baking soda
- 1 teaspoon vanilla extract
- 1½ cups all-purpose flour
- 1 teaspoon baking powder
- ¾ teaspoon salt
- ½ teaspoon ground cinnamon
- ¼ teaspoon freshly grated nutmeg
- 1 cup packed light brown sugar
- 2 large eggs

FOR SAUCE

- ½ cup (1 stick) unsalted butter
- ¾ cup packed dark brown sugar
- ½ cup heavy cream
- ⅓ to ½ cup toasted chopped pecans

Make pudding: Butter a 2½-quart soufflé dish. In a small bowl, dissolve espresso in 1 cup boiling water. Add dates and let soak 15 minutes. Stir in baking soda and vanilla.

Whisk together flour, baking powder, salt, cinnamon, and nutmeg. In another bowl, whisk brown sugar, melted butter, and eggs. Whisk sugar mixture into flour mixture until well combined. Fold in date mixture until just combined.

Pour batter into prepared dish, cover with parchment, then cover tightly with aluminum foil. Place dish in a 5- to 6-quart slow cooker. Pour enough boiling water to reach three-quarters up the sides of soufflé dish. Cover and cook on high until cake is set and a tester inserted in center comes out clean, about 2 hours (or on low for 4 hours). Transfer dish to a wire rack to cool slightly.

Make sauce: In a saucepan over low, heat butter, brown sugar, and cream until butter is melted. Bring to a boil and cook, stirring, until sauce is thick enough to coat the back of a wooden spoon, 3 to 4 minutes.

Poke holes in cake with a skewer and pour half the toffee sauce over cake. Let cake absorb some sauce. Spread sauce around evenly to soak into cake. Stir pecans into remaining sauce and serve on the side. Cake is best served warm.

A grunt, sometimes called a slump, is a classic American skillet dessert that features pillowy dumplings atop a cooked fruit filling. Think of it as a cobbler cooked on the stovetop—or in this case, in the slow cooker. The pecans are toasted in a skillet before serving, to keep them crunchy.

Peach-Pecan Grunt

SERVES 6 TO 8

4 pounds firm but ripe peaches, peeled (see page 267), halved, pitted, and cut into ½-inch wedges

1¾ cups granulated sugar

1 tablespoon cornstarch

1½ cups all-purpose flour

1½ teaspoons baking powder

½ teaspoon coarse salt

¼ teaspoon ground nutmeg

½ cup plus 6 tablespoons (1¾ sticks) unsalted butter, room temperature

1 teaspoon vanilla extract

2 large eggs

½ cup milk

1 cup pecans, coarsely chopped

¼ cup packed light brown sugar

Unsweetened whipped cream, for serving

Preheat a 5- to 6-quart slow cooker. Combine peaches, 1 cup granulated sugar, and cornstarch in the slow cooker.

In a bowl, whisk together flour, baking powder, salt, and nutmeg. With an electric mixer on medium, beat ¾ cup (12 tablespoons) butter, remaining ¾ cup granulated sugar, and the vanilla until pale and fluffy, 3 to 5 minutes. Beat in eggs, one at a time, until combined. Add flour mixture in three batches, alternating with milk, and beat until combined.

Spoon batter over peaches in cooker; smooth top with an offset spatula. Wrap slow-cooker lid tightly with a clean kitchen towel, gathering ends at top (to absorb condensation). Cover and cook on high until grunt is firm and juices are bubbling, about 3 hours (or on low for 6 hours).

Melt remaining 2 tablespoons butter in a skillet over medium. Add pecans and cook, stirring, until lightly toasted, about 5 minutes. Add brown sugar and cook, stirring, until melted, 1 minute longer. Immediately transfer to a plate to cool; break into pieces. Serve grunt topped with whipped cream and toasted pecans.

We tried all kinds of bread in testing this recipe, and brioche was the favorite, followed closely by challah. Both are dense enough to absorb all the wonderfully rich, creamy egg custard that gives this dessert its appeal.

Butterscotch Bread Pudding with Brown-Butter Rum Sauce

SERVES 8

Nonstick cooking spray

FOR BREAD PUDDING

4 large eggs, plus 1 egg yolk

¾ cup sugar

1½ cups milk, room temperature

2 cups heavy cream, room temperature

2 tablespoons unsalted butter, melted and cooled

1 teaspoon vanilla extract

Pinch coarse salt

8 cups lightly packed 1-inch cubes of day-old brioche

¾ cup butterscotch chips

¾ cup chopped pecans

FOR BROWN-BUTTER RUM SAUCE

½ cup packed dark brown sugar

4 tablespoons unsalted butter

⅓ cup whipping cream

¼ cup dark rum

Lightly coat the insert of a 7-quart slow cooker with cooking spray and preheat the cooker.

Make bread pudding: In a large bowl, whisk eggs, yolk, and sugar until well combined. Add milk, cream, melted butter, vanilla, and salt.

Add bread cubes, butterscotch chips, and pecans to slow cooker; mix to combine. Pour egg mixture over bread. Cover and cook on low until a knife inserted in center of bread pudding comes out clean, 3 hours (or on high for 1½ hours).

Remove lid and continue cooking on low until a light crust forms on top, about 30 minutes (or on high for 15 minutes). Allow bread pudding to sit uncovered at least 15 minutes before serving.

Make sauce: In a saucepan, combine brown sugar, butter, cream, and rum and bring to a boil over medium, stirring constantly. Boil, stirring constantly, until slightly thickened, 3 to 4 minutes. Pour sauce over individual servings of bread pudding.

Poaching fruit in the slow cooker actually works better than on the stovetop, because the heat is more evenly distributed. Don't toss out the flavorful poaching liquid: Boil the pear–red wine mixture into a syrup to drizzle over desserts; freeze the peach-Riesling liquid to make granita; and chill the rhubarb-rosé liquid to mix into cocktails.

Wine-Poached Pears

SERVES 6 TO 8

- 6 firm but ripe Bosc pears, stems left on, peeled
- 1 bottle (750 ml) pinot noir or other red wine
- 1 cup sugar
- 4 (1-inch) strips orange zest, removed with vegetable peeler
- 1 (3-inch) cinnamon stick, broken in half
- ½ teaspoon allspice berries

VARIATIONS

Riesling-Poached Peaches: Replace pears with 6 ripe but firm peeled **peaches** (see page 267 for peeling instructions), red wine with semi-dry **Riesling**, cinnamon with 6 **cardamom pods**, and allspice with ½ teaspoon **coriander seeds**.

Rosé-Poached Rhubarb: Replace pears with 1 pound trimmed **rhubarb**, cut into 1½-inch diagonal pieces, red wine with semi-dry **rosé**, orange zest with **lemon zest**, and cinnamon with 3 **thyme sprigs**; also, increase sugar to 1¼ cups and omit allspice. Do not bring mixture to a simmer before adding it to slow cooker.

Preheat a 5- to 6-quart slow cooker. Slice a sliver from bottoms of pears so they stand upright; nestle pears into the slow cooker.

In a saucepan, combine wine, sugar, orange zest, cinnamon stick, and allspice, and bring to a simmer. Pour over pears. Place a piece of parchment or cheesecloth over fruit to completely submerge. Cover and cook on high until tender when pierced with the tip of a knife, 2 hours (or on low for 4 hours).

Transfer pears to a large bowl. Using a sieve, strain poaching liquid over pears and refrigerate overnight.

Pour liquid into a saucepan and boil until reduced to 1 cup, about 10 minutes. Transfer to a heatproof container and let cool. Serve pears with syrup.

Stocks
&
Sauces

Applesauce,
page 262

The Basics

It is one of those line items on the to-do lists of so many home cooks: Spend some spare time making chicken stock from scratch, so you never have to rely on store-bought cans again. And yet, when the rare moments of free time present themselves, making stock is low on the list of leisure activities. (This is especially true when you're staring down the carcass of the Thanksgiving bird: After spending hours getting the feast on the table, the last place you want to find yourself is in front of the stove.) It turns out, though, that what you've needed all along is the slow cooker: Just add aromatics to the carcass (for chicken stock) or roasted bones (for beef stock), cover with water, and set on low for several hours while you go about your day.

In fact, the slow cooker may just become your secret weapon for producing a number of go-to pantry items. Take, for instance, the sauce that captures the taste and essence of late-summer tomatoes when they're at their peak, so you can enjoy them well into the fall.

The slow cooker will have you turning out recipes that you never really considered making from scratch—like ketchup and barbecue sauce; both are simple and delicious (from just long-simmered tomatoes and a handful of spices). Look to the machine for sweet pantry staples, too: It gently breaks down fresh apples into a delicious applesauce or, when combined with pears and cooked down further, a rich and complex fruit butter.

The gentle heat of the slow cooker can also coax out a food's caramelized sweetness. And to make Dulce de Leche, you need to do nothing more than pour cans of sweetened condensed milk into jars, place the jars in the slow cooker, cover with water, and set on low heat; you return hours later to find a thick caramel sauce, perfect for drizzling over ice cream, using as a dip for apple slices, or—let's be honest—eating straight out of the jar with a spoon.

Recipes

Chicken Stock

Beef Stock

Fish Stock

Roasted-Vegetable Stock

Fresh Tomato Sauce

Applesauce

Pear and Apple Butter

Dulce de Leche

Fruit Jam

Barbecue Sauce

Chile-Citrus Ketchup

Nothing beats homemade chicken stock for soups, stews, and sauces. Next time you roast a chicken, save the bones, or purchase backs and legs to use for this recipe. You can also adapt the recipe using the leftover bones from a Thanksgiving turkey.

Chicken Stock

MAKES 4 TO 5 QUARTS

2 to 3 pounds chicken bones

2 carrots, chopped

2 onions, quartered

3 celery stalks, chopped

1 leek, split lengthwise, rinsed well, and chopped

1 head garlic, cut in half

1 dried bay leaf

1 tablespoon black peppercorns

3 thyme sprigs

5 flat-leaf parsley sprigs

3 to 4 quarts boiling water

Place all ingredients except boiling water in a 6-quart slow cooker. Add the boiling water (it should cover the ingredients by 3 inches). Cover and cook on low 8 hours.

Remove from heat and strain stock through a fine-mesh sieve (discard solids). Let stock cool completely. (Stock can be refrigerated in an airtight container up to 1 week, or frozen up to 6 months.)

Unlike chicken bones, beef bones are roasted before they are used to make stock. There's nothing complicated about the process; it just adds an extra hour to the prep time. But the resulting richness and complex flavor of the stock makes it well worth the effort.

Beef Stock

MAKES 4 TO 5 QUARTS

3½ pounds beef bones, such as shanks, necks, knuckles, and shins

1 tablespoon olive oil

2 onions, quartered

2 carrots, chopped

2 celery stalks, chopped

1 head garlic, halved

3 thyme sprigs

5 flat-leaf parsley sprigs

1 dried bay leaf

6 white mushrooms

2 leeks, split lengthwise, rinsed, and roughly chopped

2 plum tomatoes, chopped

4 to 5 quarts boiling water

Preheat oven to 400°F. Combine beef bones and oil in a large bowl; toss to combine. Arrange on a rimmed baking sheet and roast about 30 minutes. Add onions, carrots, celery, garlic, thyme, parsley, bay leaf, mushrooms, leeks, and tomatoes to baking sheet, and roast until bones are deeply browned, about 30 minutes.

Using a slotted spoon, transfer bones and vegetable mixture to a 6-quart slow cooker. Add the boiling water. Cover and cook on low 8 hours. Remove from heat and strain stock through a fine-mesh sieve (discard solids). Let stock cool completely. (Stock can be refrigerated in an airtight container up to 1 week, or frozen up to 6 months.)

You'll find myriad uses for fish stock (bouillabaisse, cioppino, shrimp risotto, and more). Use the freshest bones from mild-flavored fish; avoid strong-tasting or oily fish like salmon or mackerel. You can also use fish heads in place of some of the bones. Have a fishmonger remove the gills, and be sure to rinse bones and heads well to remove any traces of blood.

Fish Stock

MAKES 4 TO 5 QUARTS

2 pounds fish bones (from non-oily, firm fish, such as snapper, sole, and bass), rinsed

1 onion, quartered

2 celery stalks, chopped

2 leeks, split lengthwise, rinsed well, and chopped

1 carrot, chopped

2 garlic cloves

3 thyme sprigs

5 flat-leaf parsley sprigs

4 quarts boiling water

Place all ingredients, except boiling water, in a 6-quart slow cooker. Add the boiling water (it should cover the ingredients by 3 inches). Cover and cook on low 8 hours.

Remove from heat and strain stock through a fine-mesh sieve (discard solids). Let stock cool completely. (Stock can be refrigerated in an airtight container up to 1 week, or frozen up to 6 months.)

It's difficult to find flavorful vegetable stock in any store—another compelling reason to make it yourself. And as with beef, roasting the vegetables makes a better-tasting stock. In this case, it's only thirty minutes in the oven before the ingredients are transferred to the slow cooker.

Roasted-Vegetable Stock

MAKES 4 TO 5 QUARTS

3 onions, quartered

5 celery stalks, chopped

3 carrots, chopped

1 head garlic, halved

1 fennel bulb, chopped

5 white mushrooms

2 leeks, split, rinsed well, and chopped

2 tablespoons olive oil

4 quarts boiling water

1 dried bay leaf

1 teaspoon black peppercorns

3 thyme sprigs

5 flat-leaf parsley sprigs

Preheat oven to 425°F. Combine onions, celery, carrots, garlic, fennel, mushrooms, and leeks in a large bowl; toss with oil. Spread in a single layer on a rimmed baking sheet and roast until golden, tossing halfway through, about 30 minutes.

Transfer vegetables to a 6-quart slow cooker. Add the boiling water, bay leaf, peppercorns, thyme, and parsley. Cover and cook on low 8 hours. Remove from heat and strain stock through a fine-mesh sieve (discard solids). Let stock cool completely. (Stock can be refrigerated in an airtight container up to 1 week, or frozen up to 6 months.)

You could certainly use this method to make tomato sauce that you plan to freeze over the winter months. But there are all kinds of reasons to use it more quickly than that. We love it as a base for the poached eggs on page 216, with pasta (naturally), and on pizza.

Fresh Tomato Sauce

MAKES ABOUT 3 CUPS

2 pounds ripe plum tomatoes, peeled cored, halved, and seeded

4 garlic cloves, smashed and peeled

¼ cup extra-virgin olive oil

4 to 5 basil sprigs

1 teaspoon coarse salt, plus more to taste

¼ teaspoon freshly ground pepper

Pinch sugar

½ cup boiling water

Preheat a 5- to 6-quart slow cooker. Add tomatoes, garlic, oil, basil, salt, pepper, and sugar to the slow cooker; stir to combine. Add the boiling water. Cover and cook on high until sauce thickens slightly, 1 hour. Reduce heat to low and cook 4 hours.

For a thicker sauce, continue cooking on low for 2 hours, or until desired thickness is reached. Use sauce immediately, or let cool to room temperature and refrigerate in an airtight container up to 3 days.

Applesauce

MAKES 8 CUPS

6 pounds apples (we like a mix
of 4 pounds McIntosh and
2 pounds Cortland or Empire),
quartered and cored (peels optional)

¼ cup fresh lemon juice

¼ cup sugar (optional)

1½ cups water

Preheat a 5- to 6-quart slow cooker.
Combine apples, lemon juice, sugar
(if using), and water in the slow cooker.
Cover and cook on low until apples are
very soft, 4 hours (or on high for 2 hours).

Pass apples through a food mill fitted
with the fine disk or a medium-mesh sieve
to remove skins. (Applesauce can be
refrigerated in airtight containers up to
1 week, or frozen for up to 3 months.)

Tip
Making pink applesauce lets you
skip the tedious step of peeling
the apples, since the color comes
from the skins.

Pear and Apple Butter

MAKES 6 CUPS

2½ pounds ripe Bartlett or
Anjou pears (about 5), peeled,
quartered, and cored

2½ pounds McIntosh or
Gala apples (about 5), peeled,
quartered, and cored

1 cup packed dark brown sugar

½ teaspoon coarse salt

1 (3-inch) cinnamon stick

Preheat a 5- to 6-quart slow cooker.

With the grating disk of a food processor,
finely grate fruit, working in batches, if necessary. Transfer fruit to the slow cooker. Stir
in brown sugar, salt, and cinnamon stick.
Cover and cook on high, 4 hours (we prefer
this recipe on high).

Remove cinnamon stick and reserve.
Transfer mixture to cleaned bowl of the
processor (in batches, if necessary)
and process until smooth. Return to slow
cooker, along with cinnamon stick, and
cook on high, uncovered, until mixture is
thick and browned, 4 hours. Discard cinnamon stick and let mixture cool. (Fruit butter
can be refrigerated in airtight containers
up to 1 month, or frozen up to 3 months.)

Dulce de Leche

MAKES 2½ CUPS

- 2 cans (14 ounces each) sweetened condensed milk
- Boiling water, for slow cooker

Preheat a 5- to 6-quart slow cooker.

Divide condensed milk among 4 half-pint canning jars (8 ounces each); secure lids and rings on each. Place jars in the slow cooker, spacing them at least 1 inch apart. Fill slow cooker with the boiling water to cover jars by 2 inches.

Cover and cook on low until desired consistency is reached, 8 to 10 hours (or on high for 4 to 5 hours); the longer the cook time, the darker the caramel becomes. Turn off heat, uncover slow cooker, and let water cool to room temperature before removing jars. Once cool, carefully remove jars, rinse, dry, and refrigerate up to 3 weeks.

Fruit Jam

MAKES ABOUT 2 QUARTS

- 3 pounds fruit (see suggestions below), cut into 1-inch chunks if large, pitted if necessary
- 1½ pounds sugar (3⅓ cups)
- 2 tablespoons fresh lemon juice
- ¼ teaspoon coarse salt

Preheat a 5- to 6-quart slow cooker. Stir together fruit, sugar, lemon juice, and salt in the slow cooker. Cook on low 2 hours. Uncover and continue cooking until jam is syrupy and beginning to thicken, 3 hours. Let cool for 30 minutes. (Jam can be refrigerated in airtight containers up to 1 month.)

Berry: 3 pounds raspberries or 1 pound each raspberries, blackberries, and strawberries (hulled)

Nectarine-Raspberry: 2¼ pounds nectarines, peeled (optional), and 12 ounces raspberries

Peach: 3 pounds white or yellow peaches, peeled (optional)

Peach-Plum: 1½ pounds each peaches, peeled (optional), and plums

Plum: 3 pounds plums

Barbecue Sauce

MAKES 4 CUPS

- 2 tablespoons safflower or canola oil
- 1 onion, finely chopped
- 3 garlic cloves, minced

  Coarse salt and freshly ground pepper
- 1¼ teaspoons chili powder
- 1 can (28 ounces) whole peeled tomatoes, pureed with their juices
- ¾ cup water, plus more as needed
- ¼ cup packed dark brown sugar
- ¼ cup ketchup
- 2 tablespoons apple cider vinegar

Preheat a 5- to 6-quart slow cooker.

Heat oil in a saucepan over medium-high. Add onion, garlic, 1 teaspoon salt, and ½ teaspoon pepper, and cook until onion is translucent, about 5 minutes. Stir in chili powder and cook until fragrant, about 1 minute. Transfer onion mixture to the slow cooker. Add tomatoes, the water, brown sugar, and ketchup. Cover and cook on high for 3 hours (or on low for 6 hours). Let cool slightly.

Transfer sauce to a blender and puree. Stir in vinegar; season with salt and pepper. Let cool completely. (Barbecue sauce can be refrigerated in an airtight container up to 2 weeks.)

Chile-Citrus Ketchup

MAKES 1 QUART

- 1 can (28 ounces) diced tomatoes
- 1 onion, quartered
- 3 garlic cloves, smashed
- 6 tablespoons dark brown sugar
- ¼ cup apple cider vinegar
- 2 teaspoons dry mustard

  Pinch ground nutmeg
- ¼ teaspoon ground allspice

  Pinch chili powder
- ½ teaspoon finely grated orange zest plus ⅓ cup fresh orange juice
- 2 tablespoons brewed espresso
- 1 dried bay leaf
- 1 fresh habañero chile

  Coarse salt and freshly ground pepper

Puree tomatoes, onion, garlic, and brown sugar in a food processor. Transfer mixture to a 5- to 6-quart slow cooker. Add vinegar, 1 cup water, mustard, nutmeg, allspice, chili powder, orange zest and juice, espresso, bay leaf, and chile. Cook, uncovered, on high until thickened, 3 to 4 hours. Remove chile. Puree half or whole chile (depending on desired heat) with 1 cup tomato mixture in food processor. Return ketchup to cooker; stir until well blended. Season with salt and pepper. Let cool completely.

Extras

Niter Kibbeh (Spiced Clarified Butter)

MAKES ABOUT 1½ CUPS

- 2 cups (4 sticks) unsalted butter, cut into small pieces
- 1 (1-inch) piece fresh ginger, peeled and grated
- 1 (1-inch) piece fresh turmeric, peeled and grated
- 2 garlic cloves, minced
- ½ small onion, finely chopped
- Pinch ground cardamom
- Pinch freshly grated nutmeg
- Pinch ground fenugreek
- ½ teaspoon ground cinnamon
- Pinch ground cloves

Melt butter in a heavy saucepan over low heat (do not let butter brown or bubble). Increase heat to medium-low and bring to a simmer. Stir in ginger, turmeric, garlic, and onion, and simmer about 2 minutes. Add cardamom, nutmeg, fenugreek, cinnamon, and cloves; reduce heat to a very low simmer for about 45 minutes. (Do not stir.) The butter will separate—a clear layer above and a milk-solid layer below. Pour off clear layer, using a spoon or ladle if necessary; discard gritty milk solids and spices. (Niter Kibbeh can be refrigerated in an airtight container up to 3 months.)

Making Breadcrumbs

Trim off crusts from a loaf of bread (Pullman, pan de mie, or other type), and tear the bread into large pieces. Pulse in a food processor to form coarse or fine crumbs, as desired. (For dried breadcrumbs, toast in a 250°F oven 12 to 15 minutes.) Breadcrumbs can be frozen, in an airtight container, for up to 3 months.

Roasting Peppers

Preheat broiler. Place 1 large red bell pepper on a foil-lined baking sheet. Broil 4 to 5 inches from heat source, about 5 minutes per side, using tongs to turn several times, until pepper is blackened and charred on all sides. Transfer pepper to a bowl, cover tightly with plastic wrap, and let stand until cool enough to handle, about 30 minutes. Peel, discarding skin, seeds, and stems. Cut pepper into 1-inch-thick strips.

Peeling Stone Fruit

The skins from stone fruits will contribute color and flavor to jam, but for a smoother mixture, you can peel them. For peaches or nectarines: Carve an X in the bottom of each and plunge them into boiling water for 30 seconds, then transfer to an ice-water bath to stop the cooking; the skins will slip off. For plums, just lift the skins out of the cooked jam with a fork.

Index